# Raspberry Pi 5 User Guide

## Master The Raspberry Pi 5
## for Creative learning and unleash its
## full potential as your New PC

Dude DD Maxwell

# Table of Contents

# INTRODUCTION

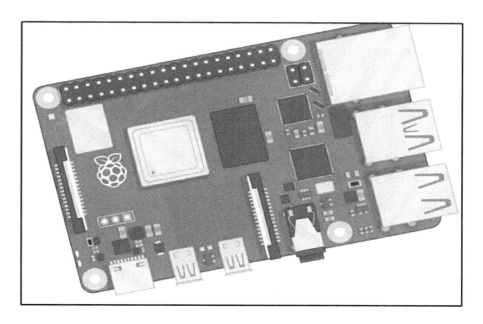

Step into the captivating realm of Raspberry Pi 5. Whether you're a tech enthusiast, a hobbyist, or a complete beginner, this versatile single-board computer is here to unlock a world of possibilities and make your journey into the realm of electronics and programming an enjoyable and rewarding experience.

The Raspberry Pi Foundation has consistently amazed us with each iteration of their flagship product, and the Raspberry Pi 5 is no exception. Designed with beginners in mind, this compact yet powerful device provides an ideal platform for learning, tinkering, and creating innovative projects.

At its core, the Raspberry Pi 5 is a credit card-sized computer that packs an impressive punch. Powered by a high-performance processor and enhanced with generous system resources, it provides a smooth and responsive computing experience. Whether you're exploring coding, building interactive projects, or simply using it as a desktop computer, the Pi 5 is up to the task.

One of the most exciting aspects of the Raspberry Pi 5 is its user-friendly nature, making it perfect for beginners. Setting up the device is a breeze, with a simple and intuitive installation process that requires no prior technical knowledge. Just connect a monitor, keyboard, and mouse, and you're ready to dive into the world of Raspberry Pi!

The Raspberry Pi 5 also supports a wide range of operating systems, including the popular Raspberry Pi OS and various Linux distributions. This flexibility allows you to choose an environment that suits your needs and preferences, ensuring a seamless transition into the world of programming and electronics.

For beginners, the Pi 5 offers an extensive library of educational resources and projects. Whether you're interested in coding with Python, exploring electronics with GPIO (General Purpose Input/Output) pins, or experimenting with sensors and actuators, the Raspberry Pi community provides a wealth of info, guides, and sample code to help you get started.

But the Raspberry Pi 5 isn't just for beginners. Its versatility and expandability make it a perfect tool for advanced users and professionals as well. Whether you're building a smart home system, a media center, or an Internet of Things (IoT) project, the Raspberry Pi 5's abundant connectivity options and vast ecosystem of accessories and add-ons ensure that you can tailor it to meet your specific needs.

The Raspberry Pi 5 is an exceptional device that opens up a world of opportunities for beginners. Its user-friendly nature, powerful performance, and extensive community support make it the ideal companion for those embarking on their journey into the realm of electronics and programming. So, grab a Raspberry Pi 5, unleash your creativity, and get ready to experience the joy of learning and making with this remarkable single-board computer!

## What a Beginner Should Know:

1. Familiarize Yourself with the Components: Before diving into the setup process, take a moment to understand the essential components of your Raspberry Pi 5. These include the board itself, an SD card for storage, power supply, HDMI cable for connecting to a monitor, keyboard, and mouse.

2. Operating System Options: Raspberry Pi 5 supports various operating systems, with Raspberry Pi OS (formerly known as Raspbian) being the most popular choice. It's a beginner-friendly OS optimized for the Raspberry Pi, offering a familiar desktop environment and a vast library of software. Other options like Ubuntu, Arch Linux, and Windows 10 IoT Core are also available for more advanced users.

## What a Beginner Should Do:

1. Prepare the SD Card: To start, you'll need to install the operating system onto an SD card. Then, follow the provided instructions to flash the image onto your SD card using a tool like Etcher.

2. Connect the Peripherals: Connect your Raspberry Pi 5 to a monitor using an HDMI cable and attach a keyboard and mouse. Ensure that the power supply is unplugged before connecting it to the board. Once everything is connected, you're ready to power up your Raspberry Pi 5.

3. Powering Up: Plug in the power supply, and your Raspberry Pi 5 will boot up. Follow the on-screen instructions to complete the initial setup, such as configuring your keyboard layout, setting up Wi-Fi, and creating a user account. Take your time to explore the interface and become familiar with the system.

## What a Beginner Should Not Do:

1. Mishandle the Components: Handle the Raspberry Pi 5 and its components with care. Avoid static electricity, physical shocks, or improper connections that may damage the board or other peripherals.

2. Overload the Power Supply: Raspberry Pi 5 requires a stable power supply. Do not use underpowered phone chargers or USB ports, as they may cause instability or damage. Always use an official Raspberry Pi power supply or a recommended alternative.

3. Overclocking without Knowledge: Overclocking is the process of running the Raspberry Pi at a higher speed than its default setting to gain more performance. However, it can lead to overheating and instability if done improperly. As a beginner, it's advisable to avoid overclocking until you have a better understanding of the system.

# GETTING STARTED WITH RASPBERRY PI 5

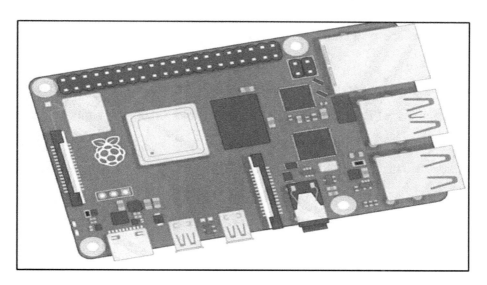

The Raspberry Pi stands apart from your typical smartphone, laptop, or desktop computer because it is built on a single printed circuit board, making it a single-board computer. This design choice is what allows the Raspberry Pi to have its compact size, just like other single-board computers.

Despite its small size, the power of the Pi 5 remains unaffected. It can perform the same tasks as larger and more power-hungry computers, albeit potentially at a slightly slower pace. Nonetheless, it gets the job done.

The Raspberry Pi family was born out of a desire to make computer education accessible on a global scale. The founders of the nonprofit Raspberry Pi Foundation couldn't have predicted the immense popularity it would achieve. In 2012, only a few thousand units were produced, and they quickly sold out. Since then, millions of Raspberry Pi devices have been sold worldwide.

People are now utilizing Raspberry Pi devices in various settings, including offices, data entry centers, classrooms, factories, homes, and even spacefaring balloons and self-piloting boats. The original Raspberry Pi was known as Model B, and subsequent models have been released with improved specifications and tailored features for specific use cases. For instance, the Raspberry Pi Zero is a smaller and more energy-efficient version of the Raspberry Pi, albeit with certain features like the wired network port and multiple USB ports removed.

All models of the Raspberry Pi are compatible, meaning that software developed for one model will work on others as well. The compatibility is so extensive that even the original pre-launch Model B prototype can run the latest version of the Raspberry Pi OS, albeit potentially at a slower speed.

This book primarily focuses on the latest and most powerful version of the Pi, the Raspberry Pi 5 Model B. However, the information provided can also be applied to other models of the Raspberry Pi, making it useful for anyone using a different Pi model.

## Guided Tour Of The Raspberry Pi

The Raspberry Pi presents all its features, components, and ports openly, unlike a traditional computer that conceals its inner workings within a case. However, you have the option to acquire a case for your Pi to provide additional protection. Through the Raspberry Pi, you'll gain valuable knowledge by observing the various parts of a computer, their functions, and how to connect additional components, also known as peripherals.

In the figure below, you can see the Raspberry Pi 5 Model B (as viewed from above). To avoid any confusion when using this book, make sure to orient the Raspberry Pi in the same way as depicted in the image, especially when working with components like the GPIO header.

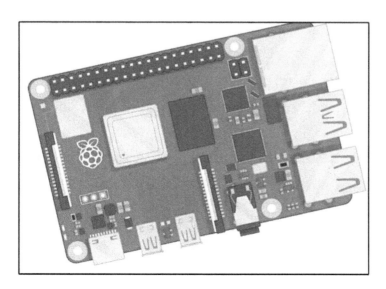

# The Raspberry Pi 5 Model B

The compact board of the Raspberry Pi may appear packed with components, but it is actually straightforward to comprehend. In this book, we will begin by exploring these components, which are responsible for the Pi's capabilities.

## The Components Of The Raspberry Pi

Similar to any other computer setup, the Raspberry Pi consists of various components, each playing a crucial role in its functionality. On the top side of the board, pay attention to the metal cap positioned just above the center. This cap houses one of the most important components: the system-on-chip (SoC).

The system-on-chip is a silicon chip located beneath the metal cover. This integrated circuit contains the majority of the Pi's system, including the central processing unit (CPU), which acts as the computer's brain, and the graphics processing unit (GPU), responsible for handling visual tasks.

Next to the system-on-chip, you'll find another chip in the form of a small, black plastic square. This chip serves as the Raspberry Pi's random-access memory (RAM). When you work on the Raspberry Pi, your data is temporarily stored in the RAM until you save it, at which point it is written to the microSD card.

The RAM and microSD card work in tandem as the Raspberry Pi's volatile and non-volatile memory, respectively. The RAM is volatile memory, meaning its contents are lost when you turn off your Raspberry Pi, while the microSD card, as non-volatile memory, retains its contents.

Another metal cap can be found at the top right of the board, housing the radio component. This radio serves two important purposes: it acts as a Wi-Fi radio, enabling the Pi to connect to computer networks, and as a Bluetooth radio, allowing the Pi to connect to peripherals like mice and exchange data with nearby smart devices such as smartphones and sensors.

Towards the bottom edge of the board, just behind the middle set of USB ports, you'll notice another black plastic-covered chip. This chip serves as the USB controller, responsible for managing the four USB ports. Adjacent to it is a smaller chip known as the network controller, which operates the Pi's Ethernet network port.

Lastly, located in the upper-left part of the board, just above the USB Type-C power connector, is the final black chip. This chip, smaller than the others, is called the power management integrated circuit (PMIC). Its role is to convert the power entering through the micro-USB port into the power required to run the Raspberry Pi.

If all of these components seem overwhelming or confusing, don't worry. Using a Raspberry Pi doesn't necessitate knowing all the specific components and their exact locations on the board.

## The Ports Of The Raspberry Pi

The Raspberry Pi is equipped with a variety of ports, including four Universal Serial Bus (USB) ports positioned along the middle and right-hand side of the board's bottom edge. These ports allow you to connect USB-compatible peripherals to your Pi, such as mice, keyboards, flash drives, and digital cameras. It's worth noting that there are two types of USB ports: those with a black interior are USB 2.0 ports, adhering to the second version of the Universal Serial Bus standards, while the ones with a blue interior are the faster USB 3.0 ports, based on the newer version three.

## The USB Ports Of The Raspberry Pi

Next to the USB ports on the right side, you'll find the Ethernet port, also known as the network port. This port allows you to connect the Pi to a wired computer network using an RJ45 connector cable. Take note of the Ethernet port, and you'll notice two light-emitting diodes (LEDs) at the bottom. These LEDs serve as status indicators, showing when the connection is active and functioning properly.

Above the Ethernet port, on the left side of the Pi, you'll see a 3.5 mm audio-visual (AV) port commonly referred to as the headphone jack. You can connect your headphones to this port, although using amplified speakers will provide better sound quality. Interestingly, the 3.5 mm AV port has an additional feature—it carries a video signal that can be connected to projectors, TVs, and other displays supporting a composite video signal. To utilize this feature, you'll need a tip-ring-ring-sleeve (TRRS) adapter, a cable specifically designed for this purpose.

Directly above the 3.5 mm AV jack, you'll find a peculiar-looking connector with a pullable plastic flap. This is the camera connector, also known as the Camera Serial Interface (CSI). It enables you to connect a specially designed Raspberry Pi Camera Module for capturing images and videos.

Moving further up the left side edge, you'll encounter the micro–High-Definition Multimedia Interface (micro-HDMI) ports. These ports are smaller versions of the connectors found on televisions, game consoles, and set-top boxes. As the name suggests, they transmit both audio and video signals, making them ideal for multimedia purposes.

You can use these ports to connect the Raspberry Pi to display devices such as computer monitors, TVs, or projectors. It's possible to connect up to two devices simultaneously.

Just above the HDMI ports, you'll find the USB Type-C power port. This port is used to connect the Pi to a power source. You may recognize the USB Type-C power port from smartphones, tablets, and other portable devices. It is recommended to use the official Raspberry Pi USB Type-C Power Supply for optimal performance, although a standard smartphone charger can also be used.

On the upper edge of the Raspberry Pi's board, there is another distinct-looking connector. At a glance, it may resemble the camera connector, but upon closer inspection, you'll notice that it is the opposite. This is the display connector, also known as the Display Serial Interface (DSI). It is specifically designed to be used with the Raspberry Pi Touch Display, allowing you to connect and interact with a touchscreen.

On the right edge of the board, there are 40 metal pins arranged in two rows with 20 pins each. This is the GPIO (general-purpose input/output) header. The Raspberry Pi utilizes these pins to transmit signals to additional hardware, such as LEDs, buttons, joysticks, temperature sensors, pulse rate monitors, and other similar devices.

Below the header, to the right, you'll find a smaller header with only four pins. This can be used to connect the Power over Ethernet (PoE), which provides an alternative power option by allowing the Raspberry Pi to be powered through a network connection rather than the USB Type-C port.

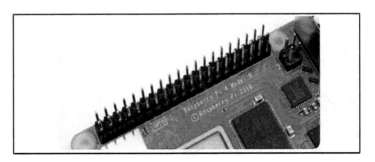

Lastly, the final port on the Raspberry Pi is not visible from the top of the board. Flip it over, and you'll discover the microSD card connector, located opposite the display connector. This is where you insert the Pi's storage—a microSD card. The microSD card serves as the storage medium for the operating system, installed software, and saved files used by the Raspberry Pi.

# The Peripherals of the Raspberry Pi

The Raspberry Pi is similar to a desktop computer in that it cannot function on its own. To use the Raspberry Pi, you need to connect it to various peripherals. At the very least, you will need a microSD card for storage, a display monitor or TV, a keyboard and mouse for input, and a power source, preferably a 5-volt USB Type-C power supply rated at 3 amps or higher. With these essentials, you can essentially have a fully functional PC. Chapter 2, "Getting Started with your Raspberry Pi," will provide more detailed instructions on how to connect these peripherals to your Pi. Additionally, there are many other peripherals that can be connected to your Raspberry Pi, expanding its capabilities.

The Raspberry Pi Foundation offers official accessories such as the Raspberry Pi case, which provides protection for your device while still allowing access to the various ports. They also provide the Raspberry Pi Camera Module, the Sense HAT for physical computing, and the Raspberry Pi Touch Display. These accessories can be connected to the display port, providing video output and a tablet-like touchscreen interface.

There are also third-party accessories available, ranging from kits that can turn a Raspberry Pi into a laptop or tablet, to add-ons that enable the Pi to understand and respond to your speech. These diverse peripherals offer exciting possibilities. However, it's important to remember that one must learn to walk before running. This means that it's advisable to first become familiar with the basic peripherals and their usage before venturing into more complex ones.

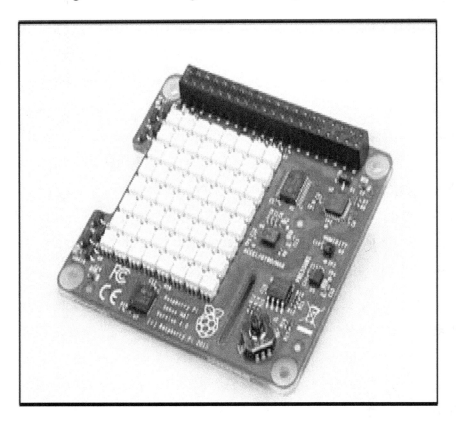

# Items Essential for Setting Up a Raspberry Pi 5

Exploring the Essential Components for Setting up a Raspberry Pi

When it comes to setting up a Raspberry Pi, there are a few key items you'll need to get started. While the Raspberry Pi may appear different from traditional closed-off computers due to its bare circuit board design, the process of setting it up is designed to be quick and straightforward. So, don't feel intimidated by its appearance!

By following the information provided in this book, you'll be able to get your Raspberry Pi up and running in under ten minutes. If you obtained this book as part of a Raspberry Pi Starter Kit, you likely already have most of the necessary components. All you'll need is a display monitor or a TV with an HDMI connection. This type of connection is commonly used in Blu-ray players, set-top boxes, and gaming consoles.

If you don't have a Raspberry Pi Starter Kit, in addition to the Raspberry Pi 5 Model B, you'll need the following items to complete your setup:

## USB Power Supply

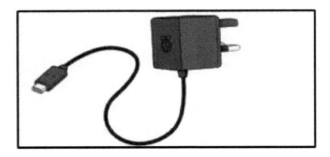

To power your Raspberry Pi, you'll need a 5V power supply with a USB Type-C connector. It's recommended to use the Official Raspberry Pi Power Supply, which is rated at 3 amps (3A). This power supply is specifically designed to handle the Raspberry Pi's fluctuating power demands effectively.

## Micro SD Card with NOOBS

The microSD card serves as the permanent storage for your Raspberry Pi. It stores all the software, files, and even the operating system. We suggest using a minimum of 16GB, but an 8GB microSD card will also suffice. It's convenient to get a card that comes with NOOBS (New Out Of the Box Software) pre-installed, as it saves you time. If you have a blank microSD card, you can find instructions on how to install NOOBS on it in Appendix A.

## USB Keyboard and Mouse

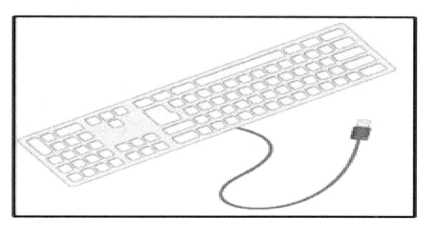

To control your Raspberry Pi, you'll need a keyboard and mouse. Any wireless or wired keyboard and mouse with a USB connector should work fine with the Raspberry Pi. However, be cautious with "gaming" style keyboards that have colorful lights, as they may draw excessive power and become unreliable. Opt for simpler keyboard and mouse options for better compatibility.

## Micro-HDMI Cable

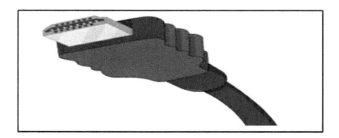

The micro-HDMI cable is necessary for transmitting both sound and images from the Raspberry Pi to a display monitor or TV. Connect the end with the micro-HDMI connector to the Raspberry Pi, and the other end with the full-size HDMI connector to the display. Alternatively, you can use a micro-HDMI to HDMI adapter along with a standard full-size HDMI cable.

If your monitor lacks an HDMI socket, you can obtain a micro-HDMI to DVI-D, Display Port, or VGA adapter. For older TVs with composite video or SCART sockets, a 3.5mm tip-ring-ring-sleeve (TRRS) audio/video cable is suitable.

Raspberry Pi Case

While it is possible to use a Raspberry Pi without a case, take caution not to place it on a metal surface. Metal conducts electricity and can potentially cause the Pi to short-circuit. It is generally recommended to use a case for added protection. The Official Raspberry Pi Case can be found in the Starter Kit, or you can explore cases made by third-party manufacturers, available from various sellers.

Wired Network Connection

If you plan to connect your Raspberry Pi to a wired network instead of using Wi-Fi, you will need a network cable to link the Pi to your network router or switch.

Wireless Network Setup

Using the Raspberry Pi's built-in wireless radio eliminates the need for a cable. However, you must be aware of the name and password or passphrase of your wireless network to establish a connection.

## Hardware Setup

To begin, unbox the Raspberry Pi. Keep in mind that while the Raspberry Pi is a robust device, it can still be damaged. Handle the board by its edges rather than the flat side, and exercise caution around the raised metal pins. Bending these pins can make it difficult to plug in add-on boards and additional hardware, and in the worst-case scenario, it can cause the Pi to short-circuit and become damaged.

## Assembling the Case

If you prefer to use a case for your Raspberry Pi, it is advisable to do this before proceeding with other steps. For the Official Raspberry Pi Case, separate the case into two parts: the red base and the white lid.

1. Hold the case's base with the elevated end on the left and the lower end on the right.

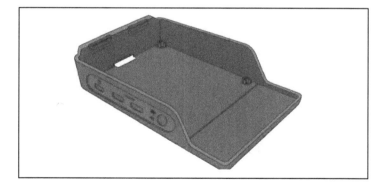

2. Ensure that no peripherals, including the microSD card, are inserted into the Raspberry Pi. Hold the Pi at a slight angle by the USB and Ethernet ports, and insert the connectors (USB Type-C, 2 × micro-HDMI, and 3.5mm) into their corresponding holes on

the side of the case. Then, lower the other side to position the Pi
flat in the base.

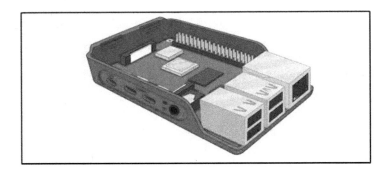

3.  Take the white lid and locate the two clips on the left side. Insert
    them into the matching holes above the microSD card slot on the
    left side of the base. Adjust until they are securely in place. Next,
    push down the right side (above the USB ports) until you hear a
    click, indicating a proper connection.

## Inserting the microSD Card

To install storage in the Raspberry Pi, you need to insert a microSD
card. If you are using a case, place the Raspberry Pi upside down.
Look for the microSD card slot labeled on the side of your Pi and

insert the card into it. The card should slide in smoothly without any resistance, fitting in only one way.

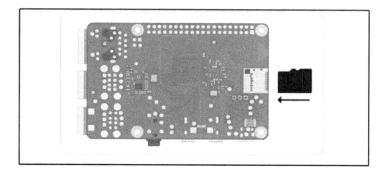

The card should slide into the connector and stop without any clicking sound.

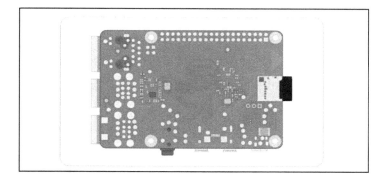

For Raspberry Pi 3 or 4, you can simply grip the protruding end of the microSD card and gently pull it out when you want to remove it. However, older Raspberry Pi models may require you to gently push the card in first to unlock it before removing it.

## Connecting a Keyboard and Mouse

You can connect your keyboard's USB cable to any of the four USB ports (2.0 or 3.0) on the Raspberry Pi. If you are using the Official Raspberry Pi Keyboard, it has a USB port on the back where you can plug in your mouse. If you are using a different keyboard, you can connect your mouse to another USB port on the Pi.

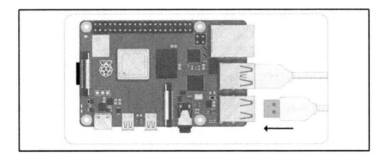

The USB connectors of the keyboard or mouse should easily slide into the USB ports. If you encounter any resistance, double-check that you are inserting the connector in the correct orientation.

Note:

### KEYBOARD & MOUSE

The keyboard and mouse act as your main means of telling the Raspberry Pi what to do; in computing, these are known as *input devices*, in contrast with the display which is an *output device*.

## Connecting a Display

When connecting a display, remember to connect the smaller end of the micro-HDMI cable to the Raspberry Pi, specifically to the micro-HDMI port closest to the USB Type-C port. Then, connect the other end of the cable to your display device. If your display has multiple HDMI ports, look for the port number next to each port and switch the input of your display to the port where you connected the Pi. If there are no port numbers, cycle through the available inputs until you find the correct one.

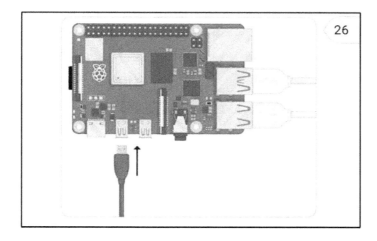

Note:

## TV Connection

If your display monitor or TV doesn't have an HDMI connector, you can still use the Raspberry Pi with it. Purchase an adapter cable from an electronics store to convert the micro-HDMI port of your Raspberry Pi to DVI-D, DisplayPort, or VGA, depending on the type of connection your display supports. Connect the adapter cable to the micro-HDMI port of your Raspberry Pi, and then use a suitable cable to connect the adapter to your display monitor.

For TVs with only composite video or SCART input, you can use a 3.5mm tip-ring-ring-sleeve (TRRS) cable.

## Connecting a Network Cable (Optional)

If you want to use a wired network connection on the Raspberry Pi, you will need an Ethernet cable, also known as a network cable. To make the connection, insert one end of the Ethernet cable into the Ethernet port of your Raspberry Pi. Ensure that the plastic clip on the cable is facing downwards, and push the cable in until you hear a clicking sound. When you want to remove the cable, squeeze the plastic clip and gently pull it out.

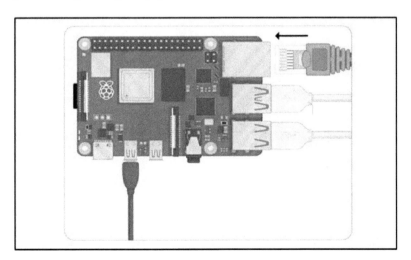

Connect the other end of the Ethernet cable to a port on your network hub in the same way you connected it to your Raspberry Pi.

## Connecting a Power Supply

The final step in setting up your Raspberry Pi is connecting it to a power supply. However, only do this when you are ready to proceed with the software installation, as the Raspberry Pi does not have a power switch and will turn on immediately when the power supply is plugged in.

Start by connecting the USB Type-C end of the power supply cable to the USB Type-C power connector of your Raspberry Pi. It should be easy since the cable can be inserted in either orientation. If you are using a detachable cable, make sure to plug the other end into the body of your power supply.

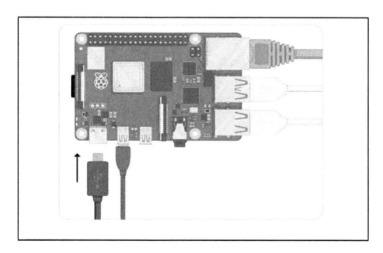

Lastly, plug the power supply into a main socket and switch on the socket. The Raspberry Pi should start up immediately.
Congratulations on successfully setting up your Raspberry Pi!

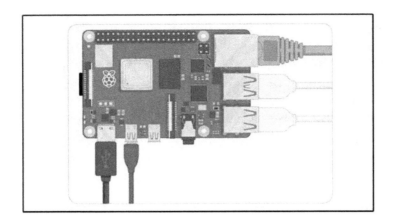

## Setting up the Software

Before you can start using your Raspberry Pi, you need to set up its software, especially the operating system (OS), which controls its operation. The NOOBS (New Out-Of-Box Software) comes in handy for this. It provides a selection of different operating systems that can be automatically installed with just a few clicks.

When you start up your Raspberry Pi for the first time with a fresh installation of NOOBS on the microSD card, you will see the Raspberry Pi logo on your screen along with a small progress window in the upper-left corner. There will be a short pause, lasting no more than a minute, during which the screen will indicate that you are using the NOOBS microSD card for the first time.

Note:

**NO PICTURE?**

If you can't see the Raspberry Pi on your display, check you are using the correct input. If your TV or monitor has more than one HDMI input, switch through each in turn using the 'Source' or 'Input' button until you see the NOOBS menu.

You are now viewing the NOOBS menu, which allows you to choose the desired operating system for your Raspberry Pi. The standard version of NOOBS includes two options: Raspbian, a version of Debian Linux designed specifically for the Pi, and LibreELEC, a version of the Kodi Entertainment Centre software.

If you prefer a different operating system, you can connect your Pi to a wired network or Wi-Fi (accessible from the 'w' option on the top bar of icons) and download/install another OS.

To install an operating system, use the mouse to check the box in front of the OS you want (for this tutorial, we'll be installing Raspbian, but

31

the instructions apply to any OS). Then, move the cursor to the white box and click the left mouse button once.

This will enable the 'Install (i)' menu icon, which was previously grayed out, indicating that the selected operating system is ready for installation.

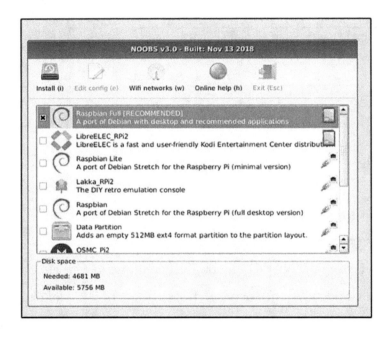

Click the 'Install (i)' icon with the left mouse button, and a warning message will appear, informing you that installing the operating system will overwrite all data currently saved on the microSD card (except for NOOBS). Click 'yes' to proceed with the installation.

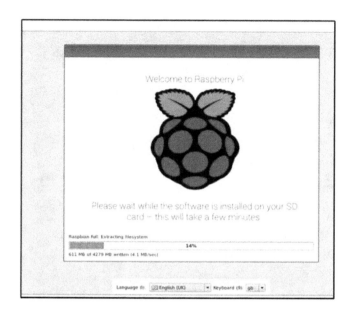

The installation process will take approximately 10 to 30 minutes, depending on the speed of your microSD card. A progress bar will be displayed at the bottom of the window, and a slideshow highlighting key features of the operating system will play. More information about the operating system will be provided in Chapter 3, "Using Your Raspberry Pi."

After the installation is complete, a window with an 'OK' button will pop up. Click the 'OK' button, and the Pi will restart into the newly installed operating system. As the Raspbian boots for the first time, you will see a series of scrolling boot messages on your screen. This is the system adjusting to the available space on your microSD card to optimize its performance. Subsequent start-ups of your Pi will be faster.

Finally, a window with the Raspberry logo will briefly appear, followed by the desktop and setup wizard.

# Using your Raspberry Pi 5

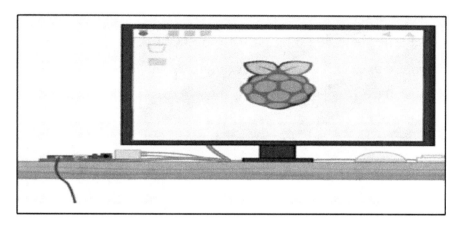

The Raspberry Pi can run a wide range of software, including different operating systems, which serve as the main software that runs a computer. One of the most popular operating systems for the Raspberry Pi is Raspbian, which is the official operating system developed by the Raspberry Pi Foundation. Raspbian is based on Debian Linux and is specifically designed for the Pi. It comes pre-installed with various extras and is ready to use.

Even if you're familiar with Apple macOS or Microsoft Windows and have never used the Raspberry Pi before, you won't encounter any difficulties with Raspbian. It follows the same principles of windows, icons, menus, and pointers (WIMP) that you're accustomed to. This chapter will help you get started and provide information about some of the included software.

## The Welcome Wizard

When you first run Raspbian, a Welcome Wizard will appear. This wizard will guide you through the process of configuring Raspbian according to your needs and location. It involves making some settings adjustments to personalize your experience.

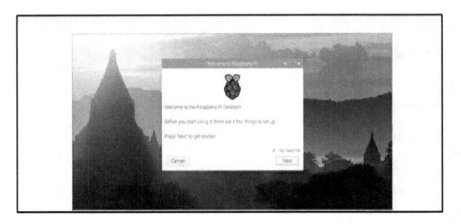

## Completing the Wizard

To close the Welcome Wizard, you have the option to click the cancel button. However, it's important to note that certain Pi features, such as Wi-Fi, may not work if you don't at least answer the first set of questions.

To proceed, click "Next" to select your country, language, and time zone. Simply click on each option and choose the appropriate answer from the drop-down box. If you're using a US-layout keyboard, make sure to check the box to ensure Raspbian uses the correct keyboard layout. Even if you're not in an English-speaking country, you can still choose to have the desktop and programs appear in English by checking the "Use English language" box. Once you're done, click "Next."

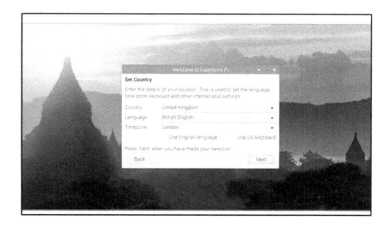

On the following screen, you'll be prompted to change the default password for the "Pi" user, which is currently set as "raspberry." Create a new password to secure your files and enter it into both boxes. You can choose to uncheck the "hide characters" option to see the password you're typing. Once you're satisfied, click "Next."

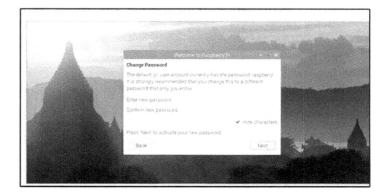

Next, you'll see a list of available Wi-Fi networks on the screen. Scroll through the list using either the keyboard or mouse and find your network's name. Once you've located it, click "Next." If your network is secure (which it should be), you'll be required to enter a password, also known as a pre-shared key. You can find this password written on the bottom of your router or on a card that came with it. Click "Next" to connect to the network or choose to skip this step if you don't want to connect.

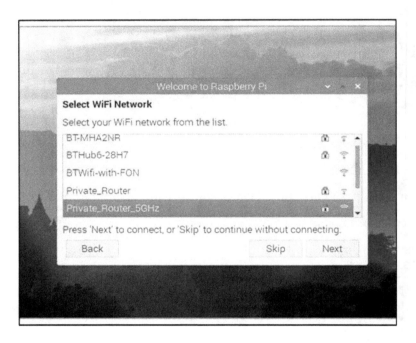

On the subsequent screen, you'll have the option to check for and install updates for Raspbian. Regular updates are provided to fix bugs, introduce new features, and enhance performance. Click "Next" to install updates or choose to skip this step if you don't want to proceed with the updates. Please note that downloading the updates may take some time. After the installation is complete, a window will appear stating that the system is up to date. Click the "OK" button.

The task on the final screen of the Welcome Wizard is straightforward. In order for certain changes to take effect, you'll need to restart, or reboot, your Pi. You will be prompted to do so, and you can click the "Reboot" button to restart your Raspberry Pi. Once you've completed these steps, the Welcome Wizard will disappear, and you can now properly use your Raspberry Pi.

## Navigating the Desktop

The version of Raspbian installed on most Raspberry Pi boards is officially called "Raspbian with the Raspberry Pi Desktop." This refers to its main graphical interface. When you access the desktop, you'll notice that a picture covers most of the screen. This picture is known as "wallpaper A," and any programs you open will appear on top of it. At the top of the desktop, you'll find the taskbar (B). This is where you can load various programs, and the loaded programs will be indicated by tasks (C) in the taskbar.

- Figure 3-7: The Raspbian desktop

| | | |
|---|---|---|
| A Wallpaper | G Network Icon | M Removable Drive Icon |
| B Taskbar | H Volume Icon | N Window Titlebar |
| C Task | I Clock | O Minimise |
| D System Tray | J Launcher | P Maximise |
| E Media Eject | K Menu (or Raspberry) Icon | Q Close |
| F Bluetooth Icon | L Wastebasket Icon | |

On the right side of the menu bar, you'll see the system tray (D). If you connect a removable storage device, such as a USB flash drive, to your Raspberry Pi, it will be displayed as an eject symbol (E). You can click on it to safely eject and remove the device. Moving further to the right, you'll find the clock (I). Clicking on it will display a digital calendar.

Next to the clock is the speaker icon (H). You can left-click on it to adjust the audio volume or right-click on it to select the audio output your Pi uses. The network icon (G) follows the speaker icon. If you're using a wireless network, a series of bars will indicate the signal strength. If you're connected to a wired network, two arrows will be displayed. Clicking on the network signal will show you a list of available wireless networks nearby. The Bluetooth icon (F) is located right next to the network icon. Click on it to view and connect to nearby Bluetooth devices.

On the left side of the menu bar, you'll find the launcher icon (J). Here, you'll find all the programs that are installed along with Raspbian. Some programs will be displayed as shortcuts, while others will be hidden in the menu. To access the hidden programs, click on the Raspberry icon (K) on the far left.

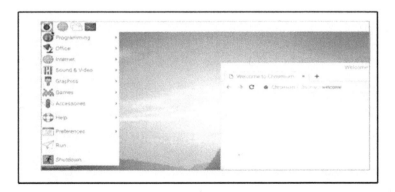

In the menu, programs are organized into categories, and the names of each category are self-explanatory. For example, the programming category contains software that will assist you in writing your own programs. "Programming with Scratch." The games category, on the other hand, includes games that you can play to pass the time. There are many more programs available besides the ones covered in this book, so feel free to experiment, explore, and expand your knowledge.

## The Chromium Web Browser

To start using the Chromium web browser on your Raspberry Pi, follow these steps:

1. Click on the Raspberry icon located at the top-left corner of your screen. This will open the menu.

2. In the menu, select the "Internet" category.

3. Click on "Chromium Web Browser" to open it.

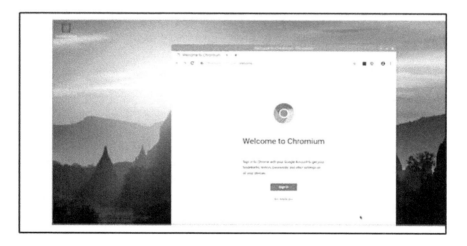

Chromium is similar to the Google Chrome browser that you may be familiar with on other computers. It allows you to visit websites, play videos and games, and communicate with people through forums and chat sites. To make the most of your screen space, maximize the Chromium window by following these steps:

1. Look at the top-right corner of the Chromium window.

2. You will see three icons in the window titlebar.

3. Click on the middle icon, which is the up-arrow icon (maximize button). This will make the window fill your screen.

If you need to minimize the window, click on the icon to the left of the maximize button. To bring the minimized window back up, click on it in the taskbar at the top of your screen. To close the window, click on the close icon located to the right of the maximize button.

## CLOSE AND SAVE

Closing a window before you've saved any work you've done is a bad idea; while many programs will warn you to save when you click the close button, others won't.

The big white bar at the top of the Chromium window, with a magnifying glass on its left side, is the address bar. To visit the Raspberry Pi website, type "raspberrypi.org" in the address bar and press ENTER on your keyboard. You can also try typing a search term, such as "Raspbian," "Raspberry Pi," or "Educational computing," into the address bar.

When you open Chromium for the first time, it may display multiple tabs along the top of its window. To open a specific tab, simply click on it. If you want to close a tab without closing Chromium itself, click on the cross icon on the right edge of the tab.

You can open multiple tabs in a Chromium window by either clicking on the tab button on the right side of the last tab or holding the CTRL key on your keyboard, then pressing the T key before releasing it.

When you are finished using Chromium, click on the close button located on the top right of the window to close it.

## The File Manager

The File Manager is a tool that helps you organize and access the files on your device. It stores various types of files, such as images, videos, and programs. To open the File Manager and access your files, follow these steps:

1. Click on the Raspberry icon at the top-left corner of your screen to open the menu.

2. Select "Accessories" from the menu.

45

3. Click on "File Manager."

Once the File Manager is open, you can browse through the files and folders on your Raspberry Pi's microSD card and any connected removable storage devices, like USB flash drives. When you open the File Manager, it automatically takes you to your home directory, which contains categorized subdirectories.

The main subdirectories in your home directory are:

- Desktop: This folder contains files that appear on your Raspberry Pi's desktop.

- Documents: Most of the files you create are saved in this folder.

- Downloads: Files downloaded from the internet using the Chromium web browser are saved here.

- MagPi: This folder stores the electronic copy of the MagPi magazine.

- Music: All music files created on the Raspberry Pi are stored here.

- Pictures: This folder contains your image files.

46

- Videos: All videos are stored in this folder, and it's the default location that video-playing programs look for.
- Public: Files saved in this folder are visible to other users of the Raspberry Pi, even if they have their own personalized accounts.

The File Manager window is divided into two panes. The left pane displays the directories available on your Raspberry Pi, while the right pane displays the files and subdirectories of the selected directory.

If you connect a removable storage device to your Raspberry Pi's USB port, a window will prompt you to open it in the File Manager. Click "OK" to access the files and directories on the device.

You can copy files between the microSD card and the removable device by dragging and dropping. To do this, follow these steps:

1. Move the mouse pointer to the file you want to copy.

2. Click and hold the left mouse button.

3. Drag the file to the other window.

4. Release the mouse button to drop the file.

Alternatively, you can use keyboard shortcuts:

- CTRL+C: Copy
- CTRL+X: Cut
- CTRL+V: Paste

## KEYBOARD SHORTCUTS

When you see a keyboard shortcut like **CTRL+C**, it means to hold down the first key on the keyboard (**CTRL**), press the second key (**C**), then let go of both keys.

To close the File Manager, click on the close button at the top-left of the window. If you have multiple windows open, close each one individually. Before unplugging a removable storage device, click on the eject button at the top-right of the screen, select the device from the list, and then unplug it.

## EJECT DEVICES

Always use the eject button before unplugging an external storage device; if you don't, the files on it can become corrupt and unusable.

The LibreOffice Productivity Suite

The LibreOffice Productivity Suite is a collection of software tools similar to Microsoft Office or Google Docs. One of the tools in the suite is LibreOffice Writer, which is a word processor. To open LibreOffice Writer, follow these steps:

1. Click on the Raspberry icon in the menu.

2. Move your mouse to the "Office" category.

3. Select "LibreOffice Writer" to launch the word processor.

In LibreOffice Writer, you can create and format documents by changing font styles, sizes, colors, adding effects, inserting pictures, tables, charts, and more. It also provides features to help you identify spelling and grammar mistakes as you type.

To practice using LibreOffice Writer, you can write a paragraph about what you have learned about the Raspberry Pi so far. You can also explore the different icons at the top of the window to see their functions. Hover your mouse over each icon to view a tooltip that explains its purpose. When you are done, go to the File menu and select "Save" to save your work with a name of your choice.

## SAVE YOUR WORK

Get in the habit of saving your work, even if you haven't finished it yet. It will save you a lot of trouble if there's a power cut and you're interrupted part-way through!

Apart from LibreOffice Writer, the LibreOffice suite includes other tools accessible from the same "Office" category in the menu. These tools are:

- LibreOffice Base: A database tool for storing and analyzing information.
- LibreOffice Calc: A spreadsheet tool for handling numbers, creating charts, and graphs.
- LibreOffice Draw: An illustration program for creating pictures and diagrams.
- LibreOffice Impress: A presentation program for creating slideshows.
- LibreOffice Math: A formula editor for creating properly formatted mathematical formulas.

LibreOffice is not limited to the Raspberry Pi and can be downloaded and installed on other computers and operating systems like Microsoft Windows, Linux, and Apple macOS. You can visit libreoffice.org to download and install it.

The Recommended Software Tool

The Recommended Software Tool is a selection of the best software available for the Raspberry Pi. It requires an internet connection to function. To access the Recommended Software Tool, follow these steps:

1. Click on the Raspberry icon in the menu.

2. Go to "Preferences."

3. Click on "Recommended Software."

The tool will download information about the available software, and a list of compatible software packages will be displayed. The software packages are categorized for easy browsing. You can click on a category in the left pane or selecta specific software package from the list to view more details.

To install a software package, follow these steps:

1. Select the software package you want to install by clicking on it.

2. Click the "Install" button.

The Recommended Software Tool will download and install the selected software package automatically. You can monitor the progress of the installation in the tool's interface.

If you want to uninstall a software package, follow these steps:

1. Click on the "Installed" tab in the Recommended Software Tool.

2. Locate the software package you want to uninstall in the list.

3. Click the "Remove" button next to the package.

The tool will uninstall the selected software package from your Raspberry Pi.

It's important to note that while the Recommended Software Tool provides a curated list of software, there are many other applications available for the Raspberry Pi that may not be included in this tool. You can explore additional software options through the Raspberry Pi's package manager or by manually downloading and installing software from trusted sources.

Remember to exercise caution when installing software and ensure that you download it from reputable sources to avoid potential security risks.

Overall, the File Manager, LibreOffice Productivity Suite, and Recommended Software Tool are valuable tools that enhance the functionality and usability of your Raspberry Pi, allowing you to efficiently manage files, create documents, and install software. Enjoy exploring and utilizing these tools to make the most of your Raspberry Pi experience!

## The Raspberry Pi Configuration Tool

The Raspberry Pi Configuration Tool is similar to the Welcome Wizard used during startup. It allows you to modify various settings available in Raspbian. Here's how to access it:

1. Click on the Raspberry icon.

2. Move your mouse pointer to the "Preferences" category.

3. Click on "Raspberry Pi Configuration" to open it.

Once the Raspberry Pi Configuration Tool is open, it is divided into four tabs, each controlling a specific aspect of Raspbian. The initial tab you see is called "System." It allows you to change your account password, set a hostname, and modify other settings.

For more detailed information about each setting, you can refer to Appendix E. It provides a comprehensive overview of the tool and its functionalities.

To access additional settings, click on the "Interfaces" tab. Here, you'll find a range of settings that are initially disabled. It's important to note that you should only change these settings if you are adding new hardware or following instructions from the hardware manufacturer.

However, there are a few exceptions to this rule:

- SSH: Enables a Secure Shell and allows you to remotely log into the Raspberry Pi from another computer on your network using an SSH client.
- VNC: Enables a Virtual Network Computer and allows you to control the Raspbian desktop from another computer on your network using a VNC client.
- Remote

## Shutting Down

When using a Raspberry Pi, it's important to properly shut it down to avoid data loss and potential system corruption. Here's what you need to know:

1. Like any computer, the Raspberry Pi stores files in volatile memory, which gets cleared when you turn off the system.

2. To ensure that your files are not lost, it's recommended to save your documents regularly. This transfers them from volatile memory to non-volatile memory, such as the microSD card.

3. Keep in mind that the files you're working on are not the only ones open in Raspbian. The operating system itself has other files open while it's running. If you abruptly disconnect the power cable while these files are still open, the operating system can become corrupted and may require reinstallation.

4. To safely shut down the Raspberry Pi, follow these steps:

i. Go to the top left of the desktop.

ii. Click on the Raspberry icon.

iii. Click on "Shutdown."

iv. A window will appear with three options: Shutdown, Reboot, and Logout.

v. Select the Shutdown option to close all opened software and shut down the Pi.

vi. Wait a few seconds after the display goes blank until the flashing green light on the Raspberry Pi turns off. Then, it's safe to turn off the power supply.

5. To turn your Raspberry Pi back on, disconnect and reconnect the power cable or toggle the power at the wall socket.

6. Rebooting the Raspberry Pi is similar to shutting it down, except it restarts the system instead of turning it off completely. You can either select the reboot option in the shutdown window or disconnect and reconnect the power cable.

7. Certain changes to your Raspberry Pi, such as installing updates or resolving software issues, may require a reboot to restart the operating system.

8. The Logout option is only relevant if you have multiple user accounts on your Raspberry Pi. Choosing this option will close any currently open programs and take you to a login screen where you'll be asked for a username and password.

9. If you accidentally select the Logout option and need to log back in, simply enter "pi" as the username and your chosen password in the Welcome Wizard, which you set up when initially configuring your Raspberry Pi.

# HOW TO SET UP A RASPBERRY PI 5 FOR THE FIRST TIME: 2$^{ND}$ METHOD

## Getting Started with Your Raspberry Pi

So, you've just received your new Raspberry Pi, whether it's the Raspberry Pi 4 or Raspberry Pi 400 and the latest version which is the pi 5, and you're ready to dive in. But where do you begin? There are countless possibilities for what you can do with this minicomputer, like setting it up as a web server or transforming it into a retro arcade. However, before you can get started, you need to set up your Raspberry Pi. Please note that if you have a Raspberry Pi Pico microcontroller, the setup process is different.

If you purchased a kit, you probably have everything you need right in the box. However, if you only have the board itself, you'll need the following items:

1. USB power adapter (such as the official Raspberry Pi 5 power supply)

2. microSD card (with a minimum capacity of 8GB, but preferably 16 or 32GB)

3. USB card reader (unless your PC already has one built-in)

Unless you plan on performing a headless install on the Raspberry Pi and controlling it remotely via a PC using remote desktop or SSH, you will also need the following:

1. Keyboard (wired or wireless)

2. Mouse or another pointing device

3. Monitor or TV

4. HDMI cables

Please note that the type of HDMI cable you need depends on the specific Raspberry Pi model you are using. Raspberry Pi 4 B, Pi 400 and pi 5 have dual micro-HDMI ports, so they require micro-HDMI to HDMI cables or adapters. Raspberry Pi Zero / Zero W and Zero 2 W have mini-HDMI ports and therefore need mini-HDMI to HDMI cables to connect to a display. All other Raspberry Pi models, including the 3 B, have standard HDMI ports and can use HDMI male to male cables to connect to your monitor or TV.

## Setting Up the Power for Your Raspberry Pi

Before you can begin setting up your Raspberry Pi, you need to ensure that it has a reliable power source. The Raspberry pi 5 is powered through a USB Type-C port. To power these models, you will need a charger that can output 5 volts and 3 amps. Most USB Type-C phone chargers may not provide enough amps, unless they support USB PD (Power Delivery). However, USB-C laptop chargers should work fine.

On the other hand, all other Raspberry Pi models, including the Raspberry Pi 3 B and Pi Zero / Zero W / Zero 2 W, are powered through a micro-USB port. This means you can power them by connecting them to various third-party chargers or even your computer's USB ports. While it's possible to provide less electricity, the optimal power source for a Raspberry Pi 5 should have 5 volts and 2.5 amps, which also ensures sufficient power for any peripherals connected to its USB ports.

There are several power supplies specifically designed for Raspberry Pis, such as the official Raspberry Pi 5 power supply and the Cana Kit 5V 2.5A supply for other Raspberry Pi models.

The Raspberry Pi does not have a built-in power switch, so the usual way to turn it on is by plugging it in. However, there are power supplies available with built-in on/off switches. It's important to note that to prevent data loss, you should use the shutdown feature in your operating system (OS) before unplugging or turning off the Pi.

## Choosing an Operating System (OS) on a microSD Card

There are numerous operating systems available for the Raspberry Pi, including the possibility of running full Windows 11 on the Pi 5. However, for most use cases, Raspberry Pi OS is the recommended choice. Raspberry Pi OS is a customized version of Debian Linux optimized for the Pi. In this guide, we will explain how to set up Raspberry Pi OS.

The Raspberry Pi does not have internal storage; instead, it boots from a microSD memory card that you provide. Make sure to get a microSD card with a minimum capacity of 8GB, preferably 32GB or higher, and ensure it has a class 10 speed rating (you can refer to our list of recommended microSD cards for Raspberry Pi). Additionally, you will need a card reader to write the OS onto the microSD card from your PC.

## Headless Install for Raspberry Pi?

If you only intend to experiment with the Pi or use it to control physical objects like lights, motors, and sensors, you don't necessarily need to connect it to a screen and keyboard. You can follow separate instructions for a headless install on the Raspberry Pi, allowing you to control the device from your PC or Mac desktop using VNC or SSH remote access software.

## Downloading and Installing Raspberry Pi OS

Once you have gathered all the necessary components, follow these steps to create the boot disk required for setting up your Raspberry Pi. These steps should work on Windows, Mac, or Linux-based PCs (we will demonstrate using Windows, but the process should be similar for all three).

1. Insert the microSD card and reader into your computer.

2. Download and install the official Raspberry Pi Imager. This application is available for Windows, macOS, and Linux, and it simplifies the process by downloading and installing the latest version of Raspberry Pi OS. Although there are alternative methods, such as downloading a Raspberry Pi OS image file and using third-party software to "burn" it onto the microSD card, using the Imager is more straightforward.

3. Click on "Choose OS."

# Raspberry Pi

4. From the OS menu, select Raspberry Pi OS (32-bit) as the preferred option (there are other choices, but for most use cases, 32-bit is recommended).

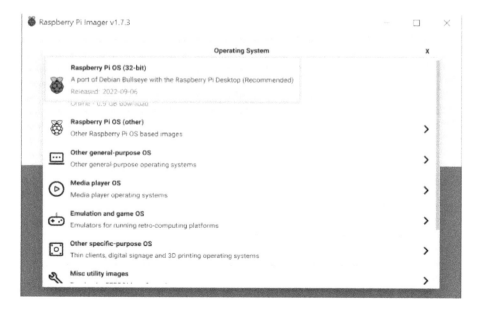

5. Click on "Choose storage" and select the microSD card you are using.

6. Click the settings button or press CTRL + SHIFT + X to access the settings.

7. Fill in the settings fields as follows and then click "Save." While these fields are technically optional, it is highly recommended to fill them out to set up your Raspberry Pi quickly and get it online without any issues. If you don't set a username and password at this stage, you will be prompted to create them through a setup wizard upon the first boot.

- Set hostname: Choose a name for your Pi, such as "raspberry pi" or any other preferred name.
- Enable SSH: Allow SSH connections to the Pi. This is recommended.
- Use password authentication / public key: Select the preferred method for logging in via SSH.
- Set username and password: Enter the username and password you want to use for the Pi.
- Configure wireless LAN: Set the SSID and password of your Wi-Fi network.
- Wireless LAN country: If you are setting up Wi-Fi, you must choose the appropriate country.
- Set locale settings: Configure the keyboard layout and timezone (usually selected correctly by default).

**Advanced options**    X

Image customization options    for this session only ▾

☑ Set hostname: myserver .local

☑ Enable SSH

  ◉ Use password authentication

  ○ Allow public-key authentication only

     Set authorized_keys for 'pi':

☑ Set username and password

  Username: pi

  Password: ••••••••

☑ Configure wireless LAN

  SSID: noc-1701

  ☐ Hidden SSID

SAVE

8. Click on "Write." The application will now proceed to download the OS and write it to your microSD card. This process may take a few minutes to complete.

# Raspberry Pi

| Operating System | Storage | |
| --- | --- | --- |
| RASPBERRY PI OS (32-BIT) | GENERIC FLASH DISK USB DEVICE | WRITE |

## Setting Up Your Raspberry Pi for the First Time

Once you have written the Raspberry Pi OS to a microSD card, it's time to boot up your Raspberry Pi and get started.

1. Insert the microSD card into the Raspberry Pi.

2. Connect the Raspberry Pi to a monitor, keyboard, and mouse.

3. If you plan to use a wired Internet connection, plug in an Ethernet cable.

4. Power on the Raspberry Pi by plugging it in.

If you had previously set up a username and password using the Raspberry Pi Imager settings, you will be taken directly to the desktop environment. However, if you did not set up these credentials, you will encounter a setup wizard.

## Using the Raspberry Pi First-Time Setup Wizard

If you chose a username and password in the Raspberry Pi Imager settings before writing the microSD card, you will be greeted with the desktop environment on the first boot. However, if you did not set up these credentials, you will be guided through a setup wizard to create a username, password, and enter network credentials. If you encounter the setup wizard, follow these steps to complete the setup of your Raspberry Pi

1. Click "Next" on the dialog box.

Welcome to the Raspberry Pi Desktop!

Before you start using it, there are a few things to set up.

Press 'Next' to get started.

If you are using a Bluetooth keyboard or mouse, put them into pairing mode and wait for them to connect.

Next

2. Set your country and language preferences, and click "Next." The default choices may already be correct.

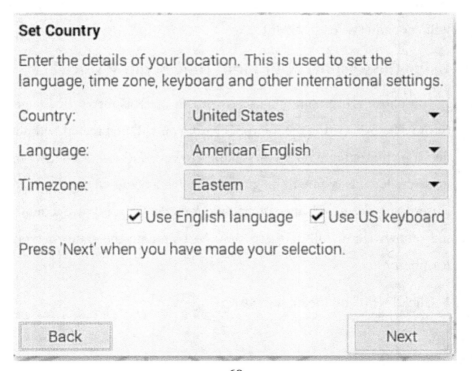

**Set Country**

Enter the details of your location. This is used to set the language, time zone, keyboard and other international settings.

Country: United States

Language: American English

Timezone: Eastern

☑ Use English language   ☑ Use US keyboard

Press 'Next' when you have made your selection.

Back                    Next

3. Enter a username and password that you would like to use for your primary login, and click "Next".

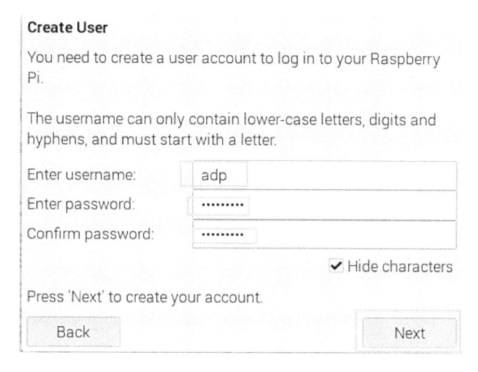

**Create User**

You need to create a user account to log in to your Raspberry Pi.

The username can only contain lower-case letters, digits and hyphens, and must start with a letter.

Enter username:      adp

Enter password:      ··········

Confirm password:      ··········

☑ Hide characters

Press 'Next' to create your account.

Back          Next

4. If the borders of the desktop are cut off, toggle the "Reduce the size of the desktop" option to "On." Otherwise, simply click "Next."

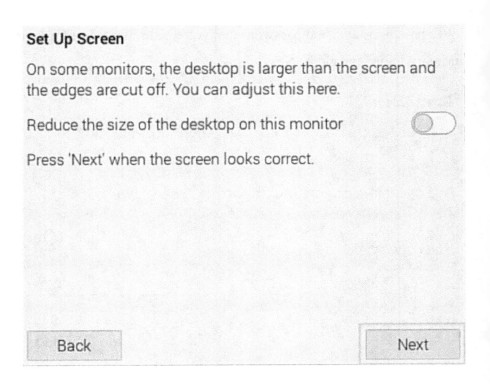

**Set Up Screen**

On some monitors, the desktop is larger than the screen and the edges are cut off. You can adjust this here.

Reduce the size of the desktop on this monitor

Press 'Next' when the screen looks correct.

Back          Next

5. If you are connecting via Wi-Fi, select the appropriate Wi-Fi network from the screen. If you are not using Wi-Fi or are using an Ethernet connection, you can skip this step.

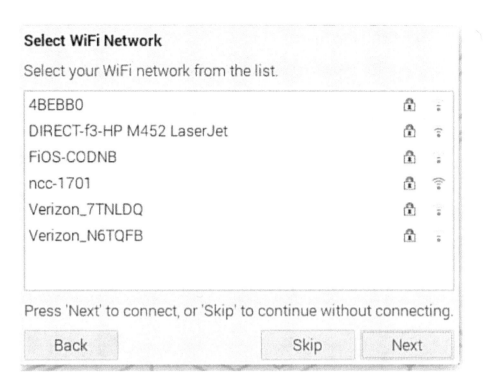

**Select WiFi Network**

Select your WiFi network from the list.

| | | |
|---|---|---|
| 4BEBB0 | 🔒 | ⋮ |
| DIRECT-f3-HP M452 LaserJet | 🔒 | 📶 |
| FiOS-CODNB | 🔒 | ⋮ |
| ncc-1701 | 🔒 | 📶 |
| Verizon_7TNLDQ | 🔒 | ⋮ |
| Verizon_N6TQFB | 🔒 | ⋮ |

Press 'Next' to connect, or 'Skip' to continue without connecting.

| Back | Skip | Next |
|---|---|---|

6. Enter your Wi-Fi password (unless you skipped the previous step because of using Ethernet).

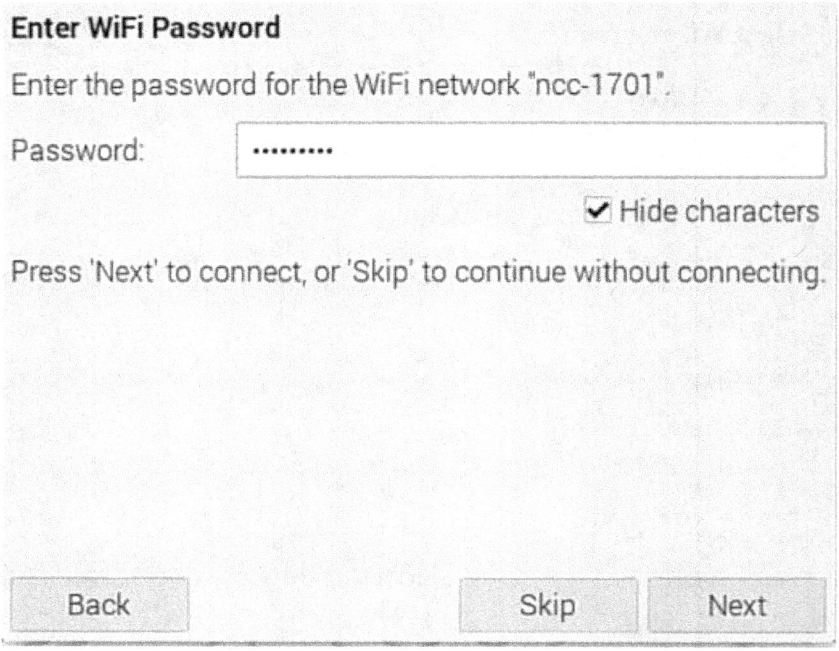

**Enter WiFi Password**

Enter the password for the WiFi network "ncc-1701".

Password:        ·········

☑ Hide characters

Press 'Next' to connect, or 'Skip' to continue without connecting.

| Back | | Skip | Next |

7. When prompted to update software, click "Next." This process requires an Internet connection and may take several minutes. If you are not connected to the Internet, you can click "Skip."

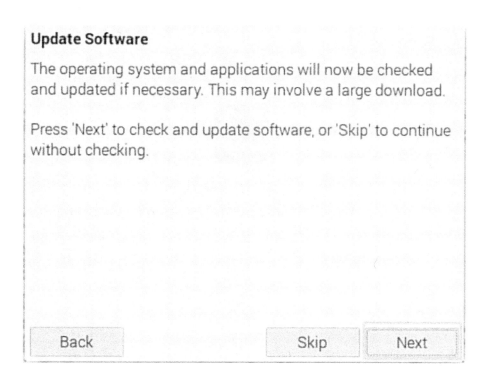

**Update Software**

The operating system and applications will now be checked and updated if necessary. This may involve a large download.

Press 'Next' to check and update software, or 'Skip' to continue without checking.

| Back | | Skip | Next |

8. Click "Restart" to complete the setup process.

**Setup Complete**

Your Raspberry Pi is now set up and ready to go.

Press 'Restart' to restart your Pi so the new settings will take effect.

| Back | | Restart |
| --- | --- | --- |

If you want to change these settings later, you can access the region and password settings, along with other options, by clicking on the Pi icon in the upper left corner of the screen and navigating to Preferences -> Raspberry Pi Configuration. Wi-Fi can be configured by clicking on the Wi-Fi/network icon on the taskbar.

## Adjusting Your Raspberry Pi's Screen Resolution

If your desktop feels cramped and you need more space, it's a good idea to change your screen resolution to match the capabilities of your display. Even if you're accessing your Raspberry Pi through VNC without a physical monitor, it's still recommended to have a minimum resolution of 720p.

To modify the screen resolution on your Raspberry Pi, follow these steps:

1. Start by opening the Screen Configuration menu. You can do this by clicking on the Pi icon and selecting Preferences -> Screen Configuration.

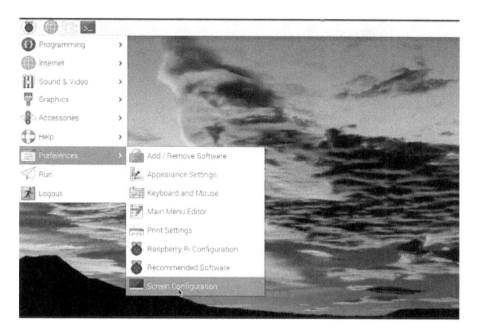

2. Once the menu is open, right-click on the HDMI box and choose your desired resolution from the Resolution menu.

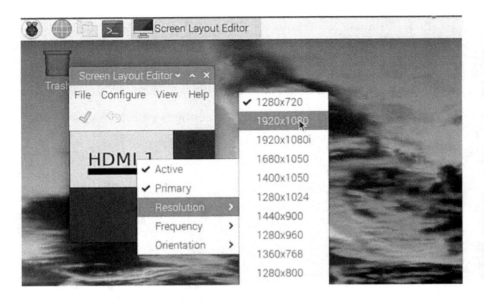

3. After selecting the resolution, check the box to apply the changes. The screen resolution will be updated accordingly.

4. Finally, click "Yes" to confirm the reboot.

Screen layout updated - changes will take effect on reboot.
Click 'Yes' to reboot now, or 'No' to reboot later

| No | Yes |

## What Can You Do Now?

Now that your Raspberry Pi is set up, the possibilities are endless! There are countless exciting projects you can explore, such as transforming your Raspberry Pi into a retro arcade machine, using it as a web server, or even utilizing it as the brain for a robot, security system, or custom IoT device. Let your imagination run wild as you discover the incredible potential of your Raspberry Pi.

# PROGRAMMING WITH SCRATCH

Utilizing the Raspberry Pi goes beyond relying solely on pre-existing software. It opens up opportunities for you to unleash your creativity by creating your own software. The Raspberry Pi provides a platform where you can develop your programs and engage in experimentation.

One tool that facilitates coding accessibility on the Raspberry Pi is Scratch. Developed by the Massachusetts Institute of Technology (MIT), Scratch is a visual programming language. It allows you to build your program step-by-step using blocks, which are pre-written sections of code represented by color-coded jigsaw pieces.

Scratch serves as a powerful and comprehensive programming environment. It empowers users to create not only simple games and animations but also complex interactive robotics projects.

# Introducing the Scratch 2 Interface

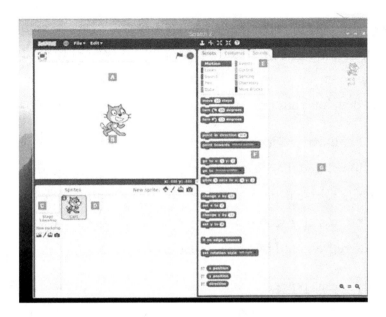

1. Stage Area: Think of the stage area as a theatrical stage where your program controls the movement of sprites (characters or objects). Sprites can be made to move around and interact with the stage.

2. Sprite: Sprites are the characters or objects that your Scratch program controls. They reside on the stage and can be programmed to perform various actions.

3. Stage Controls: The stage controls allow you to modify the stage itself and add pictures as background displays. You can customize the appearance and settings of the stage using these controls.

4. Sprites List: In the window, there is a section called the sprites list. It displays all the sprites that you have created or loaded into Scratch. It provides an overview of the available sprites for your program.

5. Blocks Palette: The blocks palette showcases all the blocks that you can use in your program. These blocks are organized into color-coded categories, making it easier to find the specific blocks you need.

6. Blocks: Blocks are pre-written chunks of program code. They provide the building blocks for your programs. By dragging and dropping blocks from the block's palette, you can construct your programs step-by-step.

7. Script Area: The script area is where you assemble your programs. You can drag and drop blocks from the block's palette into the script area to create the desired sequence of actions and behaviors for your sprites. It's the space where you build your programs using the available blocks.

## Your First Scratch Program: Hello World

To begin with Scratch, follow these steps to create your first program:

1. Loading the Scratch 2 Program:

   i. Click on the Raspberry icon to open the Raspbian menu.

   ii. Navigate to the Programming section using your cursor.

   iii. Select Scratch 2, and after a few seconds, the Scratch 2 user interface will load.

Note: Unlike most programming languages where you follow written instructions from the computer, Scratch works differently.

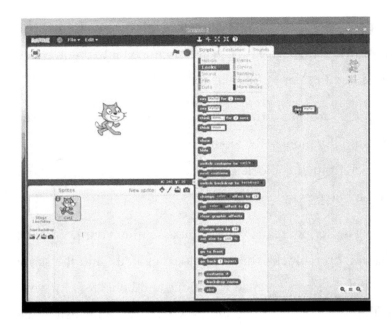

2. Getting Started with Scratch:

i. In the block's palette located at the center of the Scratch window, click on the Looks category.

ii. You will see a list of blocks available under the purple-colored category.

iii. Find the "say Hello!" block.

iv. Click and hold the left mouse button on the block.

v. Drag the block over to the script area on the right-hand side of the Scratch window.

vi. Release the mouse button to drop the block into the script area.

vii. Notice that the block has a hole at the top and a matching part sticking out at the bottom. This indicates that the block expects something above and below it. The trigger for this program is what you have above it.

3. Adding the Event:

i. Go back to the blocks palette and click on the Events category, which is light brown in color.

ii. Drag an Event block into the script area.

iii. Position the block so that the bottom part connects into the hole at the top of the "say Hello!" block. A white outline will appear.

iv. Release the mouse button to connect the blocks.

Note: The positioning doesn't have to be precise. As long as they are close enough, the blocks will snap into place like puzzle pieces. If they don't snap into place, click and hold again to adjust the position until they connect.

4. Your program is now complete and ready to run.

## To Run the Program:

To execute your program, follow these steps:

1. Go to the top of the stage area and click on the green flag icon.

2. If the program is written correctly, the cat sprite on the stage will greet you with a cheerful "Hello!" This indicates that your program is successful.

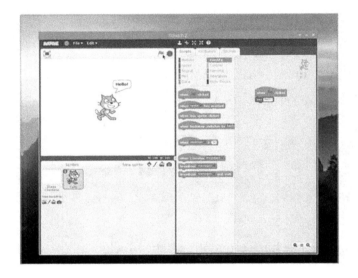

Remember to Name and Save Your Program:

Before proceeding, make sure to give your program a name and save it:

1. Click on the File menu.

2. Select "Save Project."

3. Enter a preferred name for your program.

4. Click the Save button.

## Next Steps: Sequencing

Although your program currently consists of two blocks with only one instruction to say "Hello!" when the flag is clicked, you can do more by sequencing the blocks:

1. Click and drag the "say Hello!" block from the script area back to the block's palette. This will remove the block from your program, leaving only the trigger block.

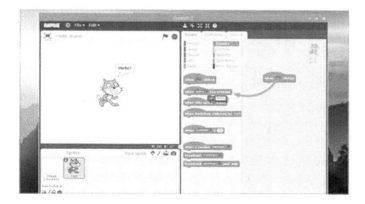

2. Go to the blocks palette and click on the Motion category. Then, click and drag the "move 10 steps" block below the trigger block in the script area. This instruction tells the cat sprite to move a certain number of steps in the direction it is currently facing.

3. To run the program, click on the green flag. The cat will move to the right and make a "meow" sound. Make sure you have speakers or headphones connected to hear the sound. Then, return to the starting position.

4. Click the flag again to repeat the action. Once the sound is repeated, it indicates that you have created a sequence of instructions for Scratch to follow, one at a time, from top to bottom.

Note: Scratch executes instructions quickly, one at a time. To modify the sequence, you can delete the "play sound meow" block until it is detached from the "done" block. Then, drag the "play sound meow" block back to the blocks palette and replace it with a simpler "play sound meow" block. Afterward, drag the "move 10 steps" block back to the bottom of the program.

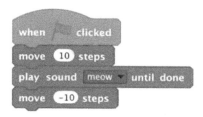

To run the program again, click on the green flag. You may notice that the cat sprite doesn't seem to move. However, the sprite is actually moving very quickly, almost instantly, back to its starting position. This happens because the "play sound meow" block doesn't wait for the sound to finish before moving to the next step. Raspberry Pi processes instructions quickly, causing the cat sprite to appear motionless.

To address this, you can use a different method to create a delay between instructions. Follow these steps:

1. Click on the Control category in the block's palette, which is color-coded in gold.

2. Click and drag a "wait one sec" block between the "play sound meow" block and the bottom "move 10 steps" block.

3. Select the green flag to run the program one last time.

4. Now, you will notice that the cat sprite waits for a second after moving to the right before moving back to the left. This delay allows you to control the timing of your sequence of instructions.

## Looping the Loop

In the previous section, we created a sequence that ran only once when the green flag was clicked. It caused the cat sprite to move and meow, but the program stopped until the green flag was clicked again.

However, we can avoid this stoppage by utilizing a special type of block in Scratch called the LOOP.

To create a looping program, follow these steps:

1. Go to the blocks palette and select the Control category, which is color-coded in gold. Look for the "forever" block.

2. Click and drag the "forever" block to the script area. Place it below the "when clicked" block and above the first "move 10 steps" block.

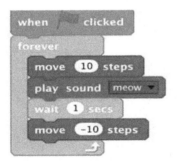

Once you've done this, you will notice that the C-shaped "forever" block automatically surrounds the other blocks in your sequence. When you click the green flag, your program will run continuously in a loop instead of running once and stopping.

This process is known as an infinite loop in programming, where the loop keeps recurring indefinitely. To stop the infinite loop, click on the red octagon located next to the green flag above the stage area.

If you want to change the type of loop, follow these steps:

1. Click and drag the first "move 10 steps" block, as well as the blocks beneath it, out of the "forever" block. Drop them below the "when clicked" block.

2. Then, click and drag the "forever" block to the blocks palette to delete it. Afterward, click and drag the "repeat 10" block below the "when clicked" block. Place it around the other blocks.

To run the new program, click on the green flag. It may appear that the program is performing the same actions as the original version, continuously repeating the sequence of instructions. However, in this case, instead of running indefinitely, the loop will end after ten repetitions. This is known as a definite loop, where you have control over when it finishes.

Utilizing loops, both infinite and definite loops, is highly beneficial for many programs, including sensing programs and games.

## Variables and Conditionals

Understanding variables and conditionals is crucial for coding your Scratch programs effectively.

In programming, a variable is a value that can change over time and is controlled by the program. A variable consists of two properties: its name and the value it stores. It's important to note that the value of a variable can be more than just a number. It can also be text, a true or false value, or even empty (null). In games, variables are often used to track things like the speed of moving objects, the current level being played, the health of a character, or the score. These are all examples of variables.

Here's how you can work with variables in Scratch:

1. Click on the File menu and select "Save Project" to save your existing program.

2. If you want to start a new and blank project, click on "File" and then select "New."

3. Go to the blocks palette and click on the "Data" category.

4. Select the "Make a Variable" button.

5. Enter "loops" as the variable name.

6. Click "OK" to create a series of blocks related to the variable.

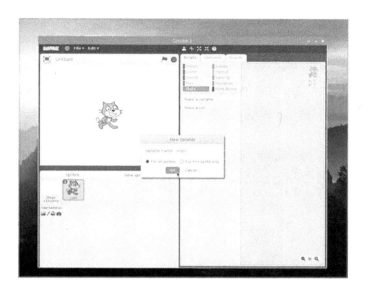

7. Click and drag the "set loops to 0" block onto the script area. This sets the variable to initialize with a value of 0.

8. Go to the Looks category in the blocks palette and drag the "say Hello! for 2 secs" block below the "set loops to 0" block.

9. Instead of manually writing the message in the "say Hello!" block, you can use variables. To do this:

10. Click on the Data category in the block's palette again.

11. Click and drag the rounded "loops" block, which is a reporter block with a tick box next to it, from the top of the list. Place it over the word "Hello!" in the "say Hello! for 2 secs" block. This will create a new combined block called "say loops for 2 secs."

12. Go to the blocks palette and click on the Events category.

13. Click and drag the "when green flag clicked" block to the top of your sequence of blocks.

14. Click on the green flag above the stage area, and the cat sprite will say "0," which is the initial value assigned to the variable "loops."

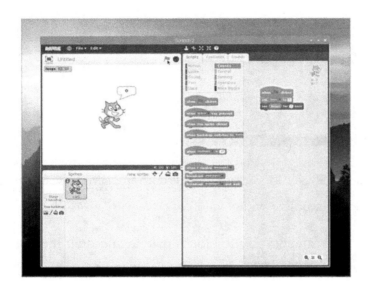

Variables can do more than just being modified. Let's explore some additional functionalities:

1. Click and drag the "say loops for 2 secs" block to detach it from the "repeat 10" block. Place it below the "repeat 10" block.

2. Click and drag the "repeat 10" block to the blocks palette to delete it. Replace it with a "repeat until" block. Make sure to connect this block to the bottom of the "say loops for 2 secs" block. Surround both blocks in your sequence.

3. Go to the blocks palette and select the "Operators" category (green color). Click and drag the diamond-shaped block and drop it into the corresponding hole in the "repeat until" block.

The operator block allows you to compare two values, including variables. Let's try it out:

1. Click on the "Data" category in the block's palette.

2. Drag the "loops" reporter block into the first empty square of the Operator block.

3. Click on the second empty square.

4. Type the number "10".

5. Click on the green flag above the stage area.

You will notice that the program works similarly to before, with the cat sprite counting from 0 up to 9 before stopping. This happens because the "repeat until" block functions similarly to the "repeat 10" block. However, instead of counting the number of loops itself, it compares the value of the "loops" variable to the specified value. Once the "loops" variable reaches 10, it stops. This is an example of a comparative operator that compares two values.

Now let's explore comparative operators using the other diamond-shaped blocks:

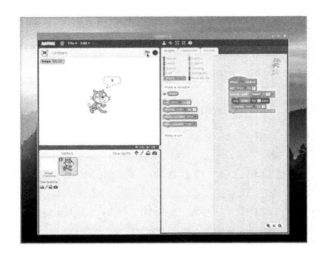

1. Go to the blocks palette and click on the "Operators" category.

2. You will see two additional diamond-shaped blocks above and below the one with the "=" symbol. These are comparative operators. The "<" compares two values and triggers if the value on the left is smaller than the one on the right. The ">" is triggered when the value on the left is greater than the one on the right. Let's see how they work:

3. Go to the blocks palette and click on the "Control" category.

4. Find the "if-then" block.

5. Click and drag it to the script area below the "say loops for 2 secs" block.

6. This will automatically surround the "change loops by 1" block. Click and drag it to connect it to the bottom of the if-then block instead.

7. Click on the "Looks" category in the block's palette.

8. Click and drag a "say Hello! for 2 secs" block and place it inside the if-then block.

9. Click on the "Operators" category in the blocks palette.

10. Click and drag the "n>n" block into the diamond-shaped hole in the if-then block.

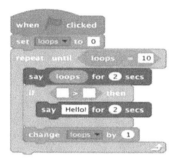

The if-then block represents a conditional block, where the blocks inside it only run if certain conditions are met.

1. Go to the blocks palette and click on the "Data" category.

2. Drag and drop the "loops" reporter block into the first empty square of the symbol block.

3. Click on the second empty square.

4. Type the number "5".

5. Lastly, click on the word "Hello!" in the say Hello! for 2 secs block.

6. Type "That's high!"

7. Click on the green flag to run the program.

The program will work similarly to before, with the cat sprite counting from zero upwards. When the number reaches 6, which is greater than 5, the if-then block will be triggered, and the cat sprite will comment on how high the numbers are getting. By following these instructions, you now have a good understanding of variables and conditionals.

# PROJECT 1--ASTRONAUT REACTION TIMER

- The Astronaut Reaction Timer is a project created in honor of British ESA astronaut Tim Peake and his time aboard the International Space Station.

- If you want to keep your existing program, it is recommended to save it. Then, click on "File" and select "New" to start a new project.

- Before starting, give your project a name by clicking on "File" and selecting "Save project." You can name it "Astronaut Reaction Timer."

- Please note that this project requires two images: one for the stage background and another for the sprite. These images are not included in Scratch's built-in resources.

- To download these images, follow these steps:

i. Click on the raspberry icon to open the Raspbian menu.

ii. Move the mouse pointer to "Internet."

iii. Click on "Chromium Web Browser."

iv. Once the browser loads, enter "rpf.io/astronaut-backdrop" in the address bar.

v. Press the ENTER key.

vi. Right-click on the space picture.

vii. Click on "Save image as..."

viii. Select the "Download" folder.

ix. Click the "Save" button.

x. Next, click on the address bar again and type "rpf.io/astronaut-sprite."

xi. Press the ENTER key.

xii. Right-click on Tim Peake's picture.

xiii. Click on "Save image as..."

xiv. Select the "Download" folder.

xv. Click the "Save" button.

- Once you have saved both images, you can choose to close Chromium or leave it open. You will use it in the taskbar to switch back to Scratch 2.

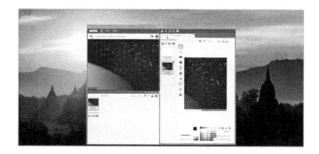

- Now, let's get started with the following steps:
- Right-click on the cat sprite located on the stage.
- Select "Delete" to remove it.
- At the bottom-left of the Scratch 2 window, you will find the stage controls.
- Click on the upload backdrop icon.
- Go to the "Downloads" folder and select the file "Space-background.png."
- Click "OK" to confirm.
- The plain white background will be replaced with the space picture, and the scripts area will be replaced with the backdrops area. For now, click on the "Scripts" tab at the top of the Scratch 2 window.

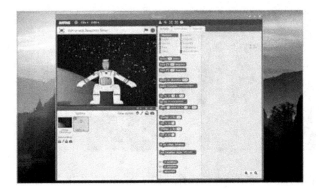

- Next, click on the upload sprite icon located next to the "New sprite" option at the top of the sprites pane.

- Search for the file "Astronaut-Tim.png" in the "Downloads" folder.

- Click on it to select it and then click "OK." The sprite will automatically appear on the stage, but it may not be in the center. Use your mouse to click and drag the sprite to place it near the lower middle.

- Now that you have a new background and sprite in place, you can start creating your program. Follow these steps:

- Create a new variable called "time" and make sure to select "For all sprites" before clicking "OK."

- Click on your sprite, either on the stage or in the sprite pane, to select it.

then add a (when clicked) block from the Events category to the scripts area. Next, add a (say Hello! for 2 secs) block from the Looks category, then click on it to change it to say 'Hello! British ESA Astronaut Tim Peake here. Are you ready?'

Add a (wait 1 secs) block from the Control category, then a (say Hello!) block. Change this block to say 'Hit Space!', then add a (reset timer) block from the Sensing category. This controls a special variable built into Scratch for timing things, and will be used to time how quickly you can react in the game.

Add a (wait until) Control block, then drag a (key space pressed?) Sensing block into its white space. This will pause the program until you press the **SPACE** key on the keyboard, but the timer will continue to run – counting exactly how long between the message telling you to 'Hit Space!' and you actually hitting the **SPACE** key.

You now need Tim to tell you how long you took to press the **SPACE** key, but in a way that's easy to read. To do this, you'll need a (join) Operators block. This takes two values, including variables, and joins them together one after the other – known as *concatenation*.

- Finally, drag an "Operators" block into the blank space in the middle. Then, drag a "distance" reporting block into the newly created blank space.
- Note that the "round" block rounds numbers up or down to the nearest whole number, avoiding hyper-accurate or difficult-to-read values for kilometers.

- To run your program, click on the green flag. Observe how far the ISS will travel in the time it takes to press the SPACE key. Remember to save your program when you are done so that you can easily load it again without starting over.

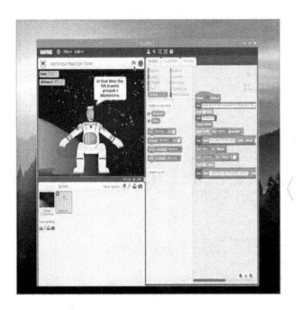

# PROJECT 2--SYNCHRONIZED SWIMMING

- The purpose of this project is to demonstrate that games can utilize more than one button for control. It offers two-button control using the ← and → keys on the keyboard.
- To start, create a new project and save it as "Synchronized Swimming."
- Go to the stage control section and click on "Stage."
- Select the "Backdrops" tab.
- Choose a water-like blue color from the palette.
- Click on the white backdrop.

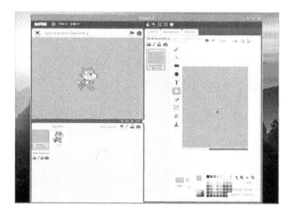

- Right-click on the cat sprite and choose "delete."
- To access a list of built-in sprites, click on the "choose sprite from library" icon.

- Select the "Animals" category and then choose "Cat1 Flying." Click "OK." Note that this sprite is also suitable for swimming projects.

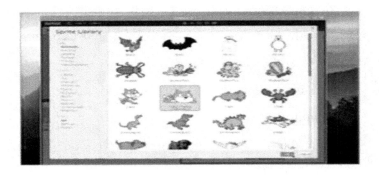

- Click on the new sprite and drag two "when space key pressed" events block into the scripts area.
- Click the small down arrow next to the word "space" on the first block and select the "left arrow" from the options.
- Drag a "turn 15 degrees" motion block underneath the "when left arrow pressed" block.
- Repeat the previous step with the second event block, but this time choose the "right arrow" from the options and use a "turn 15 degrees" motion block.
- To test your program, press the ← or → keys. You will see that the cat sprite turns as you move in the chosen direction on the keyboard. Note that you don't need to select the green flag because the event blocks you used are always active, even when the program is not running.

- Repeat the same steps twice, but this time choose the "up arrow" and "down arrow" for the event trigger blocks and use a "move 10 steps" motion block. Now press the arrow keys, and you will see that the cat can turn around and swim both forward and backward.
- Scratch has a feature called "costume" that allows you to change the appearance of the cat sprite to make its motion more realistic. Follow these steps to do so:
- Click on the cat sprite.
- Above the block's palette, click on the "Costumes" tab.
- Select the "cat1 flying-a" costume.
- Click on the round X icon at the top right corner to delete it.
- Choose the "cat1 flying-b" costume and use the name box at the top to rename it to "right."
- Rename the costume to "right" on this copy and select it.
- Click on the flip left-right icon and right-click on the newly renamed "right" costume.
- Select "duplicate" to create a copy.
- Click and rename the copy to "left."
- By following these instructions, you will have two costumes for your sprite: one named "right" where the cat faces the right, and the other named "left" where the cat faces the left.

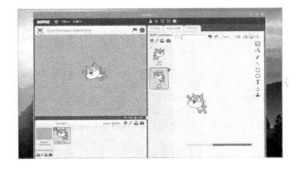

- Go to the "Scripts" tab above the costume area.

- Drag two "switch costume to" blocks from the "Looks" category below your "left arrow" and "right arrow" event blocks.

- Change the block under the "right arrow" event block to "switch costume to right."

- Give the arrow keys a try again. You will notice that the cat turns to face the direction it is swimming.

- In the case of Olympic-style synchronized swimming, where more swimmers are needed, the position of the cat sprite must be reset. Follow these steps:

- Add a "when clicked" event block.

- Add a "go to x: 0 y: 0" motion block underneath, and adjust the values if needed. Also, add a "point in direction 90" looks block.

- Select the green flag.

- Now you will see that the cat moves to the middle of the stage while facing right.

- To create more swimmers, add a "repeat 6" block, adjusting the default value of 10. Inside the block, add a "create clone of myself" control block.
- To make the swimmers swim in different directions, add a "turn 60 degrees" block above the "create clone" block, still inside the "repeat 6" block. Select the green flag and try using the arrow keys to see the swimmers come to life.
- To add music and complete the Olympic feeling, follow these steps:
- Click on the "Sounds" tab above the block's palette.
- Select the "choose new sound from library" icon.
- Choose the "Music Loops" category.
- Play the small icons until you find your preferred music.
- Click "OK" to select the music.
- Click on the "Scripts" tab to open the scripts area again.
- Add another "when clicked" event block to your script area.

- Add a "forever" control block.

- Inside the control block, add a "play sound until done" block and search for the chosen music.
- Test your program by clicking on the green flag.
- To stop the music, click on the red octagon, which will stop the program and silence the sound.
- Lastly, you can simulate a full dancing routine by adding a new event trigger to your program. Follow these steps:
- Add a "when space key pressed" event block.
- Add a "switch costume to right" block below it.
- Below that, add a "repeat 36" block, adjusting the value if needed. Inside the block, add a "turn 10 degrees" block and a "move 10 steps" block.
- Start the program by clicking on the green flag and press the SPACE key to try the new routine.
- Save your program when you're done.

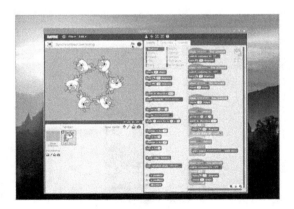

# PROJECT 3--ARCHERY GAME

The Archery game is about trying to hit a moving target using a bow and arrow.

To start, follow these steps:

1. Open the Chrome Web browser.
2. Type in rpf.io/archery-resources and press ENTER. It'll take a moment to download the game resources.
3. Switch back to Scratch 2.
4. Select the File menu and choose Load Project.
5. Go to the Places pane on the left side and click on "Pi."
6. Click on the "Downloads folder."
7. Open the ArcheryResources.sb2 file by clicking the "Open" button.
8. You may be asked if you want to replace your current project. If you haven't saved your changes yet, click Cancel and save them. Otherwise, select OK.

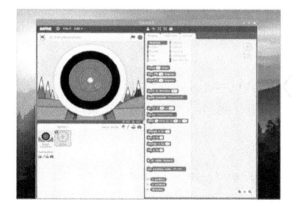

Note that your new project only has a backdrop and a sprite without any game code. You'll need to add the code yourself:

1. Add a "when clicked" block.
2. Add a "broadcast message 1" block.
3. Click the down arrow at the end of the block and choose "New Message."
4. Type "new arrow" and click OK. Now your block should say "broadcast new arrow."

Broadcasting is like sending a message that any part of your program can receive. To make use of this broadcast:

1. Add a "when I receive new arrow" block.
2. Below that, add a "go to x: -150 y: -150" block and set the size to 400%.

Now, when you click the green flag, you'll see the arrow sprite move to the bottom-left of the stage and quadruple in size.

To add a challenge where the arrow moves randomly:

1. Drag a "forever" block, followed by a "glide 1 secs to x: -150 y: -150" block.
2. Change the first box in the glide block to "0.5."
3. Use a "pick random -150 to 150" block in the other two white boxes.

Click the green flag again, and you'll see the arrow drifting around the stage.

However, there's no way to lose the arrow at the target yet. To fix this:

1. Drag a "when space key pressed" block.
2. Also, add a "stop all" block.
3. Change it to "stop other scripts in sprite" by selecting the down arrow at the end of the block.

# PROGRAMMING WITH PYTHON

The term "Python" comes from the Monty Python comedy group and now refers to a popular computer programming language.

Python is widely used worldwide for building dynamic applications and solutions. Unlike Scratch, Python isn't based on visual blocks but on text. This makes Python's text-based simulation practical and convenient.

With Python, you write instructions using specific language and syntax that your computer can understand.

If you've spent time experimenting with Scratch, Python is a natural progression. It offers more flexibility and a traditional programming experience.

You might worry that learning Python is hard, but it's not. With practice, you can start by writing simple programs, like basic calculations. As you gain confidence and mastery, you can progress to creating more complex applications, such as games and 3D environments.

# Introducing the Thonny Python IDE

Toolbar: Thonny Python's toolbar is designed with simple mode modules and features attractive icons on its menu bar. These icons are easy to understand, each representing a different function such as saving, creating, loading, and running programs in various ways.

Script area: Your Python programs are written in the script area, which is usually divided into two parts - the main area and a smaller supplementary area. The main area occupies most of the space and acts as a canvas for your programs. It also includes a side margin that displays line numbers for reference.

Python shell: This is where you run your code and set options for how your programs should execute. Additionally, you can input individual instructions here, which are executed as soon as you press the ENTER key.

Variable area: This section provides convenience and easy tracking of all changes, whether intentional or unintentional. Think of it as a log of your sessions when you create and run programs.

## Your First Python Program: Hello, World!

If you're looking to open Thonny from the menu, you can find it easily by locating its unique icon. Just like other applications installed on the Raspberry Pi, Thonny stands out with its distinct icon. Simply click on the Raspberry icon, navigate to the programming section, and select Thonny Python IDE. Give it a moment to load, usually in its simple mode, and you'll be greeted with its user-friendly interface.

Thonny is essentially an Integrated Development Environment (IDE) that brings together all the necessary tools for designing, writing, or developing software into one cohesive user interface. Unlike other IDEs that support multiple programming languages, Thonny focuses on supporting just one language, making it a specialized tool.

One of the notable differences when using Python is the lack of visual feedback as you write programs, unlike Scratch which offers real-time graphics. You'll find Python's traditional approach of writing hard lines of code more appealing compared to the modern interfaces of other IDEs.

To start your first program, click on the Python shell area located at the bottom-left of the Thonny window. Type the following instruction and hit ENTER:

```python
print ("Hello, World!")
```

Once you hit ENTER, your program will run instantly. If you see 'Hello, World!' displayed, your program has run successfully. This happens because the interpreter has examined your code, found it valid, and executed it. The entire process, displayed in the shell area, is known as the interactive mode, similar to a face-to-face interaction where communication involves sending, processing, and receiving information.

## Syntax Error

Coding becomes engaging when your programs run just as you've designed them. However, it can be frustrating when you encounter a 'syntax error' message and can't figure out what went wrong. Typically, this message pops up in the shell area, indicating that there's an issue with your code. Whether you've missed a bracket, a quotation mark, or accidentally added extra symbols to 'print,' your program won't run until the code is corrected.

To fix this, simply retype the instruction, ensuring it matches exactly with the example provided in this book, and then press ENTER.

Next, click on the script area located on the left-hand side of the Thonny window and retype your program:

```python
print("Hello, World!")
```

After hitting ENTER, you'll notice no changes except for a visible blank line in the script area. To test your program, click on the Run icon in the Thonny toolbar. A prompt will appear, asking you to save your session. Use a descriptive name like "Hello World" and click the save button. Once your program is saved, two messages will appear in the shell area.

The first message is a command from Thonny, instructing the interpreter to load the program you just saved. The second message is the output of your program.

Congratulations! By executing your first program using both interactive and script models, you've officially become a coder.

## Challenge: Creating New Messages

Now that you've learned to run programs using both interactive and script methods, you might encounter some challenges when trying to change the message displayed by the Python program. You might also struggle to determine the best method for adding new messages. You may wonder what happens if you remove brackets or quotation marks from the code and run it.

### Next Steps: Loops and Code Indentation

Python organizes functions and strings using a technique called indentation. This system ensures that your programs are interpreted correctly.

To create a new program, click on the new icon in the Thonny toolbar. A new tab will appear above the previous one, allowing you to run new programs while still working on the other. You can start with the following instruction:

```python
print ("Loop starting!")

for i in range (10):

```

The output you see on the first line in the shell area is similar to the feedback from the Hello World program. The second output initiates a definite loop, similar to Scratch, where 'i' is assigned a series of numbers. The loop starts at 0, goes up to 9, but never reaches 10. The colon symbol (:) indicates that the instructions following it belong to the loop and will be executed accordingly.

Python uses indentation to achieve similar functionality, but it does so in a different way. Indenting your code is essential in Python and makes your code clear, with each instruction having a specific place in the sequence. Failing to implement or understand this concept can result in errors and confusion.

## Challenge: Change the Appearance

To create engaging content for your end users, consider using images to add fun, much like other popular culture references such as Halloween costumes. You can create a prank using colors and images to provide an enjoyable experience with a picture. You can create your own spot-the-difference or scary images using a graphics editor like GIMP. Additionally, you can enhance the challenge by implementing tracking measures to verify users who correctly identify the differences.

# PROJECT 1: TURTLE SNOWflAKES

Now that you've got a grasp of how Python functions, it's time to add some graphics and create a snowflake using a tool called a turtle.

Physical robots often mimic the natural movements found in the environment, especially those of animals. In the wild, a turtle, just like its digital counterpart, moves in a straight line, makes turns, and coordinates its limbs minimally. Imagine this motion on your screen, where the turtle draws a line from one point to another. While some languages like Logo and its variations have a built-in turtle tool, Python doesn't. However, Python offers a vast library of add-on code that makes the turtle's movements quite practical.

Libraries consist of sets of code that introduce new instructions and variables, expanding Python's capabilities. By using an import command, you can start creating impressive content with this skill.

To create a new program and test your skills in this area, click on the new icon and type the following:

```python

import turtle
```

When you utilize data from a library, it's important to follow a syntax arrangement. You'll need to use the library name followed by a full stop, and then the instruction. Typing this out every time can be tedious, so you can assign a shorter variable name instead, preferably a single letter that also serves as a nickname for the turtle. Type the following:

pat = turtle. Turtle ()

To see how your program works, you'll need to give your turtle a task. Type the following:

pat.forward(100)

Click the Run icon and save your program as "Turtle Snowflakes." Once you've done this, a new window titled 'Turtle Graphics' will appear. Here, you'll get a preview of your program: your turtle, Pat, will move forward 100 units, drawing a straight line.

## Pat is drawing a line!

When you switch back to the Thonny window from the graphics canvas, you might not easily spot it because it's usually in the background. To find it, move your cursor to the minimize function and click it. Alternatively, you can go to the taskbar at the top of the screen, where you'll find the stop button to close the Turtle Graphics window.

Typing out each movement instruction by hand would be tiresome, so let's simplify things. Delete line 3 and create a loop to handle the task of carving out shapes:

for i in range (2):

    pat.forward(100)

    pat.right(60)

    pat.forward(100)

    pat.right(120)

Run your program, and Pat will draw a single parallelogram.

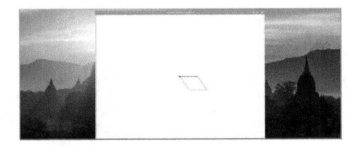

To turn this into a snowflake-like shape, click the Stop icon in the main Thonny window and modify your loop by adding another loop around it. Replace line 3 with:

for i in range (10):

Then add the following at the bottom of your program:

    pat.right(36)

Your program won't run as it is because the existing loop isn't indented correctly. To fix this, click at the start of each line in the existing loop (lines 4 through 8) and press the SPACE key four times to correct the indentation. Your program should now look like this: import turtle

Click the Run icon, and watch as the turtle draws a parallelogram as before. However, when it's done, it'll turn 36 degrees and draw another, and then another, until there are ten overlapping parallelograms on the screen, resembling a snowflake.

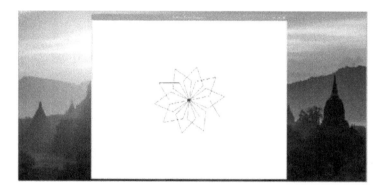

While a robotic turtle draws in a single color on a large piece of paper, Python's simulated turtle can use a range of colors. Add a new line 3 and 4,

pushing the existing lines down: import random

Change the background color from 'blue' to 'grey' in line 4, then create a new variable called 'colours' while adding a new line 5:

colours = ["cyan", "purple", "white", "blue"]

## U.S. SPELLINGS

Many programming languages, including Python, default to American English spellings. For instance, in line 5, the command should be spelled "color" rather than "colour." Using British spellings can cause your program to fail. However, this rule doesn't apply to words associated with variables, where you have the freedom to choose your own semantics.

Continuing with the example from line 5, this type of variable is called a list, and it's marked by square brackets. In the case of our snowflake, it specifies colors. But you still need to instruct Python to choose a color each time the loop repeats. At the end of the program, add the following line, making sure it's indented with four spaces so it's part of the outer loop:

```
pat.color(random.choice(colours))
```

Click the Run icon, and behold as the snowflake-stroke-ninja-star is magically drawn. This time, Python will select a random color from your list for each petal, giving the snowflake a pleasing, multicolor finish.

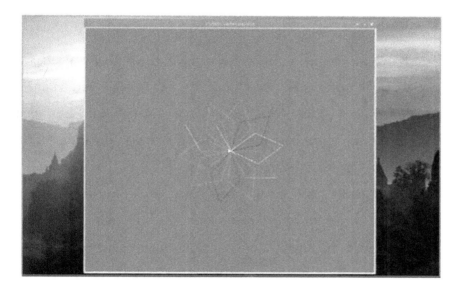

Using random colors for the 'petals'

Now that you can create a ninja star, it's time to write code that brings to life a gentle snowflake, resembling those in real life. To achieve this, add a new line 6 directly below your colors list with the following instructions:

```
pat.penup()
```

pat.forward(90)

pat.left(45)

pat.pendown()

The "penup" and "pendown" instructions move a simulated pen off and on the graphics page, much like working with a paper surface. Instead of using a loop, as you've been doing, you're going to create a function that can be called when needed. This function will remain in your portfolio.

To start, delete the code for drawing your parallelogram-based snowflakes. That includes everything from the "pat.color("cyan")" instruction on line 10 through to "pat.right(36)" on line 17. But don't touch the "pat.color(random.choice(colours))" code. Instead, add a hash symbol (#) at the start of the line. Using a hash creates a comment, which Python ignores when interpreting the code. You can also use comments to add explanations to your code for clarity, especially when revisiting it later or sharing it with others.

To create a function, you first need to define it. Let's define our function called 'branch' by typing the following instruction in line 10, just below 'pat.pendown()':

def branch ():

This instruction defines your function and sets the values you want in the 'branch' container. When you press ENTER, Thonny will automatically include indentation for the function's instructions. Pay

126

close attention to the indentation, as a misplaced blank space could affect your nesting efforts.

Type the following instructions below the function definition:

```
for i in range (3):

    for i in range (3):

        pat.forward(30)

        pat.backward(30)

        pat.right(45)

        pat.left(90)

        pat.backward(30)

        pat.left(45)

        pat.right(90)

        pat.forward(90)
```

Make sure that the new loop you create remains above the commented-out color line. You should also run and call your new function:

```
for i in range (8):

    branch ()

    pat.left(45)
```

Your finished program should look like this:

```python
import turtle

import random

pat = turtle.Turtle()

turtle.Screen().bgcolor("grey")

colours = ["cyan", "purple", "white", "blue"]

pat.penup()

pat.forward(90)

pat.left(45)

pat.pendown()

def branch ():

    for i in range (3):

        for i in range (3):

            pat.forward(30)

            pat.backward(30)

            pat.right(45)

            pat.left(90)

            pat.backward(30)

            pat.left(45)

            pat.right(90)
```

```
    pat.forward(90)

for i in range (8):

    branch ()

    pat.left(45)

#   pat.color(random.choice(colours))
```

Click on Run and observe the graphics window as Pat implements your instructions. Congratulations! Your snowflake now looks a lot more like a real snowflake.

## Challenge: What's Next?

Can you use the commented-out instruction to draw the branches of the snowflake in different colors? Can you create a 'snowflake' function and use it to draw lots of snowflakes on the screen? Can you have your program change the size and color of the snowflakes randomly?

# PHYSICAL COMPUTING WITH RASPBERRY PI

Physical computing involves writing programs that interact with hardware to produce physical actions, such as movement or activation. An everyday example of physical computing is your washing machine. You turn it on, set the temperature or spinning rate, and it performs physical actions in response to your commands.

Learning about physical computing becomes much easier with the help of Raspberry Pi – a useful tool for mastering physical computation. Its primary component is the general-purpose input/output (GPIO) header.

## Introduction to GPIO Header

The GPIO header sits at the top edge of the Pi circuit board and resembles two rows of metal pins. It serves as a connection point for hardware components like light-emitting diodes (LEDs) and switches, allowing them to interact with the programs you've written to produce physical computing outputs.

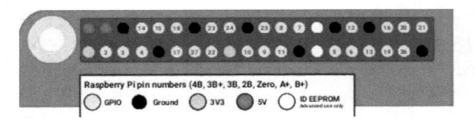

Although the name might seem complex, it aptly describes its function. The GPIO pins can be used for both input and output purposes, making them versatile. When these pins are exposed like this, they are referred to as a header, hence the name: General-purpose input/output header.

The Raspberry Pi GPIO header contains 40 male pins, some of which are available for physical computation, while others provide power or are reserved for add-on hardware like the Sense HAT.

Pin types are categorized based on their functions, each serving a specific purpose.

| 3V3 | 3.3 volts power | A permanently-on source of 3.3 V power, the same voltage the Raspberry Pi runs at internally |
|---|---|---|
| 5V | 5 volts power | A permanently-on source of 5 V power, the same voltage as the Raspberry Pi takes in at the micro USB power connector |
| Ground (GND) | 0 volts ground | A ground connection, used to complete a circuit connected to power source |
| GPIO XX | General-purpose input/output pin number XX | The GPIO pins available for your programs, identified by a number from 2 to 27 |
| ID EEPROM | Reserved special-purpose pins | Pins reserved for use with Hardware Attached on Top (HAT) and other accessories |

When working with Raspberry Pi's GPIO header, caution is crucial. Avoid bending the pins when connecting or disconnecting hardware. Never connect two pins simultaneously unless instructed to do so in a project. Connecting two pins at once can result in a short circuit, potentially causing permanent damage to the Pi.

## Electronic Components

To start your physical computing journey, you'll need a few key items, including the GPIO header and other electrical components that can be controlled through it. While there are many different components available, most GPIO projects use these common parts.

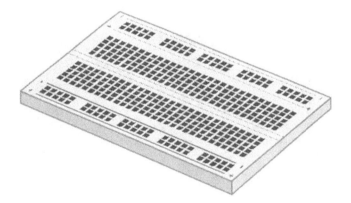

Breadboard: This makes physical computing much simpler. With a breadboard, you don't have to worry about connecting multiple component wires manually. Its metal tracks beneath the surface allow for easy connections. Breadboards also provide power distribution, making circuit creation a breeze. While it's not absolutely necessary, using a breadboard can save you a lot of hassle. It's often referred to as "solderless."

Jumper Wires: These wires connect your electrical components to the Raspberry Pi. There are three types of jumper wires: M2F (male-to-female), which are used to connect components to the GPIO pins via a solderless connection; F2F (female-to-female), which allow for individual component connections without a solderless setup; M2M (male-to-male). Depending on your project, you may need all three types of jumper wires, although M2M and M2F can be skipped if you're using a solderless setup.

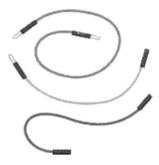

Push Button Switch: Also known as a momentary switch, this type of switch is commonly found in game console controllers. It typically comes with either 2 or 4 terminals, both of which work well with the Raspberry Pi. The push button acts as an input device, allowing you to trigger specific actions in your program. Another type of switch is the latching switch, which requires you to hold down the button for activation. Once activated, a latching switch remains in its toggled state until toggled again.

## Light-Emitting Diode (LED):

The LED works differently from the push-button. It's an output device that can be controlled directly by your program. When it's turned on, it emits light. LEDs are commonly found in various places around buildings, from small ones to large ones. They come in different shapes, sizes, and colors. However, not all LEDs are suitable for use with the Raspberry Pi. Some are designed to work with 12V or 5V power supplies, so it's best to avoid using them.

## Resistors:

Resistors are responsible for controlling the flow of current and come in different values measured in ohms ($\Omega$). The resistance of resistors is determined by the number of ohms they have. In Raspberry Pi physical computing projects, resistors are often used to protect LEDs from receiving too much electric current, which could damage them. For added flexibility, you'll need a 330-ohm resistor.

## Piezoelectric Buzzer:

Also known as a sounder, the buzzer is an output device, but unlike an LED, it produces sound instead of light. A piezoelectric buzzer contains two metal plates that vibrate against each other when activated, producing a buzzing noise. There are two types of buzzers: active and passive. An active buzzer is the preferred choice for your physical computing projects.

Motors are another important component that requires a special control board to connect to the Pi. Infrared sensors detect temperature, humidity sensors, and movement. Additionally, Light-Dependent Resistors (LDRs) are input devices that function similarly to reverse LEDs.

Various retailers worldwide offer components for physical computing with the Raspberry Pi, either individually or in kits that provide everything you need to get started. Some popular retailers include:

- RS Components (uk.rs-online.com)
- CPC (cpc.farnell.com)
- ModMyPi (modmypi.com)
- Pi Hut (thepihut.com)
- PiSupply (uk.pi-supply.com)
- Adafruit (adafruit.com)
- Pimoroni (pimoroni.com)

To complete the projects, you'll need at least:

- 3 LEDs: green, yellow, and red or amber
- 2 push-button switches

- 1 active buzzer

- Male-to-female (M2F) and female-to-female (F2F) jumper wires

- Optionally, a breadboard and male-to-male (M2M) jumper wires.

## Reading Resistor Color Codes

Resistors come in various values, from tiny wire-like ones with zero resistance to larger ones comparable to a human leg in size. However, only a few resistors have their values written visibly, usually indicated by colored bands on the resistor itself.

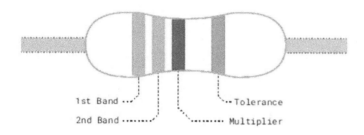

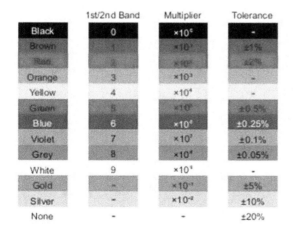

| | 1st/2nd Band | Multiplier | Tolerance |
|---|---|---|---|
| Black | 0 | ×10⁰ | - |
| Brown | 1 | ×10¹ | ±1% |
| Red | 2 | ×10² | ±2% |
| Orange | 3 | ×10³ | - |
| Yellow | 4 | ×10⁴ | - |
| Green | 5 | ×10⁵ | ±0.5% |
| Blue | 6 | ×10⁶ | ±0.25% |
| Violet | 7 | ×10⁷ | ±0.1% |
| Grey | 8 | ×10⁸ | ±0.05% |
| White | 9 | ×10⁹ | - |
| Gold | - | ×10⁻¹ | ±5% |
| Silver | - | ×10⁻² | ±10% |
| None | - | - | ±20% |

To read the value of a resistor, you need to look at the bands. Position the bands so that the first ones are on the left and the lone band is on the right. The first step is to identify the colors of the first and second bands, which correspond to the first and second figures of the resistor value. In this example, both orange bands have a value of '3', so together they make '33'. If your resistor has more than three bands, note the value of the third band (for resistors with five or six bands, refer to rpf.io/5-6band).

Next, examine the last set of bands and identify the color of either the third or fourth band. This color corresponds to the 'Multiplier' section, indicating the number by which you multiply the current value to get the correct resistor value.

For example, a brown band represents '$x10^1$' in scientific notation, meaning you add a zero to the end of the number. A blue band represents '$x10^6$', indicating you add six zeros to the end of the number. So, if the orange bands represent '33' and you add the zero from the brown band, it becomes '330': the resistor's value measured in ohms.

The final band on the right serves as a tolerance indicator for the resistor. Cheaper resistors usually have a silver band, indicating their value might vary by up to 10% higher or lower. Absence of a band means it can vary by up to 20%. More expensive resistors have grey bands, indicating they're within 0.05% of the actual rating. For hobbyist projects, such precision isn't usually necessary.

Values of resistors over 1000 ohms are measured in kiloohms (k$\Omega$), and those over 1 million ohms are called megohms (M$\Omega$). So, a 2200

Ω resistor would be indicated as 2.2 kΩ, while a 2200000 Ω resistor would be indicated as 2.2 MΩ.

# YOUR FIRST PHYSICAL COMPUTING PROGRAM: HELLO, LED

Creating an LED light marks the beginning of your journey into learning physical computing, much like writing 'hello world' is the traditional start to learning programming. For this project, you'll need an LED with a 330-ohm resistor, or a resistor with a rating close to 330 ohms, along with female-to-female (F2F) jumper wires.

## Resistance Is Important:

The resistor is crucial in the circuit as it acts as a safeguard for both the LED and the Raspberry Pi. It limits the electrical current flow that the LED draws, preventing it from receiving too much current, which could cause damage. Without the resistor, there's a risk of the LED burning out or damaging the Pi. This resistor, often called a current-limiting resistor, usually has a value of 330 ohms, which works well for most LEDs.

The resistor's value affects the LED's brightness: higher resistor values result in dimmer LEDs, while lower values make them brighter. It's important not to connect the Pi and the LED directly without the current-limiting resistor, unless the LED already has a built-in resistor of the required value.

Getting Started:

To begin, ensure your LED is functional. Position the Raspberry Pi so that the GPIO header is split into two vertical columns on the right. Connect one end of a F2F jumper wire to the Raspberry Pi's 3.3V pin.

Using another F2F jumper wire, connect the other end to the longer leg (anode or positive) of your LED. Then, use a third F2F jumper wire to connect the shorter leg (cathode or negative) of the LED to the first ground pin.

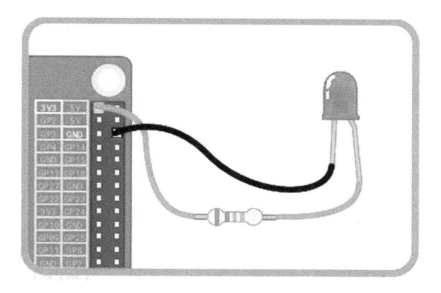

Testing Your Setup:

Once your Raspberry Pi is powered on, the LED should light up. If it doesn't, double-check your connections to ensure everything is correct. Verify that the resistor value isn't too high for your LED or the Raspberry Pi.

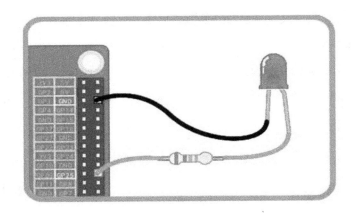

Programming:

After confirming the LED is functional, it's time to program. Disconnect the F2F jumper wire from the 3.3V pin and connect it to GPIO pin 25. The LED will turn off, which is normal.

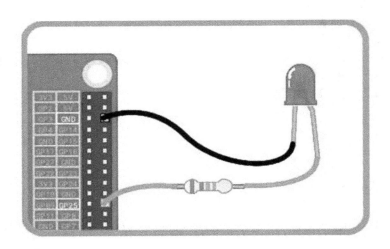

## Coding Knowledge:

To proceed with programming, you'll need to be comfortable using the Thonny Python IDE. Chapter 4 contains projects that will help you become familiar with it, so be sure to review them before continuing with this project.

# LED CONTROL IN PYTHON

To access Thonny, navigate to the programming area of the Raspberry menu. Click on the "NEW" button to start a new project and save it as "Hello LED." For this project, you'll need to use a library called GPIO Zero to interact with the GPIO pins from Python. Specifically, we'll only need a part of this library to work with LEDs. To import this part of the library, enter the following code into the Python shell section:

from gpiozero import LED

Next, you need to specify to GPIO Zero which GPIO pin is connected to the LED. Write the following code:

led = LED (25)

These lines allow Python to control LEDs connected to the Pi's GPIO pin 25. If you have more than one LED in your circuit, you'll need to use the following code to control them:

led.on()

To turn off the LED, use:

led.off()

Congratulations! You can now control the Raspberry Pi's GPIO pin using Python. Try writing these codes again. Note that if the LED is already off, `led.off()` won't have any effect, and the same goes for `led.on()` when the LED is already on.

To create a functional code, input the following into the script section:

```
from gpiozero import LED from time import sleep

led = LED (25)

while True:

    led.on()

    sleep (1)

    led. Off ()

    sleep (1)
```

This code imports the LED from the GPIOZero library and the sleep function. It then creates an infinite loop to turn the LED on for one second and off for another second continuously. Press the "Run" key to see the LED flashing.

## Challenge: Increasing the Light-Up Duration

To modify the program to make the LED stay on or off for a longer period, adjust the sleep function's duration. The sleep function controls the duration of time the LED stays on or off.

# USING A BREADBOARD

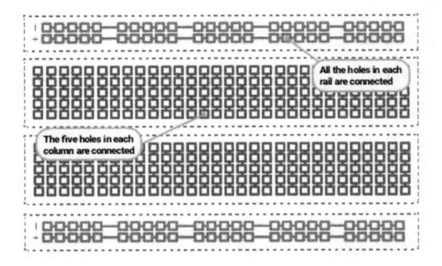

Breadboards are designed with holes that match the size of the components, typically 2.54 mm apart. Beneath these holes are metal strips, acting as the connections similar to the jumper wires we've been using. These strips run in rows across the breadboard, with a gap down the middle separating them into two sections.

Most breadboards are labeled with letters along the top and numbers along the sides, such as A1, B1, B2, etc. For instance, A1 represents the hole in the top left corner, while B1 is the hole immediately to the right, and so on. The metal strip underneath connects A1 to B1, and similarly, the first hole in each row is connected to the second hole unless you add a jumper wire.

On larger breadboards, there are additional strips of holes along the sides, often colored red, blue, or black. These are called power rails, making the wiring process much simpler.

To provide a ground for many features of the breadboard, connect a wire from the Pi's ground pin to one of the power rails, typically marked in blue, red, black, or with a minus sign (-). Similarly, if your circuit requires 3.3V or 5V power, connect a wire from the corresponding pin on the Pi to the appropriate power rail.

Adding electronic components to a breadboard is straightforward: align their leads (the metal parts) with the holes and gently push them into place.

When connecting components, you may need to extend beyond what the breadboard offers. You can use male-to-male (M2M) jumper wires to connect from the breadboard to the Pi, or female-to-male (M2F) jumper wires to connect components directly to the GPIO pins.

Remember not to insert more than one jumper wire or component lead into a single hole on the breadboard. Since the holes are connected in rows except for the separation down the middle, a component lead inserted into A1 is electrically connected to anything you add to B1, C1, D1, and so on.

# READING A BUTTON

When you see the "input/output" section of the GPIO, it means that the pins can be used for both input and output functions. For this project, you'll need a breadboard, male-to-male (M2M) and male-to-female (M2F) jumper wires, along with a push-button switch. If you don't have a breadboard, you can use female-to-female (F2F) jumper wires, but it might be trickier to press the button without disrupting the circuit.

Start by adding the push-button switch to the breadboard. If your push-button has two legs, ensure they are placed in different rows on the breadboard. For a push-button with four legs, position it so that the legs align with the holes on the breadboard, with the smooth sides facing the top or bottom.

Connect the ground rail to the ground pin on the Raspberry Pi using an M2M jumper wire. Then, connect one leg of your push-button switch to the ground rail using another M2M jumper wire.

Finally, connect the second leg of your push-button switch, if it's a four-legged switch, to the GPIO 2 pin on the Pi using an M2F jumper wire.

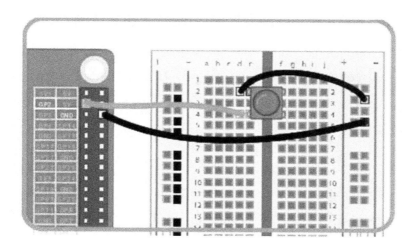

## Reading a Button in Python

To start a new project in Thonny, click the "New" button and then save it by clicking on the "Save" button, naming it "Key Input." Using a GPIO as an input for a button is quite similar to using a pin as an output for an LED. The main difference lies in importing a part of the GPIO Zero library. Here's how to set it up:

from gpiozero import Button

button = Button (2)

To execute the code when the button is pressed, GPIO Zero offers the `wait_for_press` function. Simply add the following line:

button.wait_for_press()

print ("You pushed me!")

Now, click the "Run" button and press the push-button. Your input will be displayed in the Python shell at the bottom of the Thonny window. If you wish to rerun the program, simply click the "Run" button again. The program will stop once the message is printed because it doesn't contain a loop.

For expanding your program to include an LED and resistor back in the circuit, make sure to connect GPIO pin 25 to the resistor and the longer leg of the LED. The shorter leg of the LED should connect to the breadboard's ground rail.

If you want to control the LED and read a button simultaneously, it's important to import the Button and LED functions from the GPIO Zero library, along with the sleep function. Here's how to set it up:

from gpiozero import LED, Button

from time import sleep

button = Button (2)

led = LED (25)

Replace the line `print ("You pushed me!")` with the following code to control the LED:

led.on()

sleep (3)

led.off()

Your final program should look like this:

```
from gpiozero import LED, Button

from time import sleep

button = Button (2)

led = LED (25)

button.wait_for_press()

led.on()

sleep (3)

led.off()
```

Press the "Run" button and press the push-button: the LED will turn on for three seconds, then turn off. Now you can control an LED using Python.

## Challenge: Adding a Loop

To add a loop to repeat the program, wrap the code in a while loop. You'll need to make changes to ensure the LED stays on when not clicked and turns off when clicked.

# MAKE SOME NOISE: CONTROLLING A BUZZER

LEDs are great for output, but if you're looking for something different, consider using a buzzer. It produces audible noise, which can be useful in various projects.

For this project, you'll need male-to-female (M2F) jumper wires, a breadboard, and a working buzzer. If you don't have a breadboard, you can still connect the buzzer using female-to-female (F2F) jumper wires.

Programming and circuitry for an active buzzer are similar to those for an LED. You can use the same circuit setup as you did for the LED, but replace the LED with the active buzzer. Unlike the LED, the buzzer doesn't need a resistor because it requires more current to operate.

Connect one leg of the buzzer to GPIO 15 and the other leg to the ground pin (marked as GND) using the breadboard and M2F jumper wires.

If your buzzer has three legs, mark the one with a minus sign (-) and connect it to the ground pin. Label the leg marked "SIGNAL" or "S" and connect it to GPIO 15. The remaining leg should be connected to the 3.3V pin (labeled 3V3).

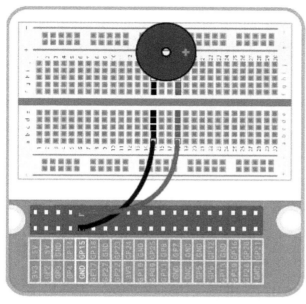

## Controlling a Buzzer in Python

To control an active buzzer using the GPIO Zero library in Python, the process is similar to controlling an LED. You'll have states like ON and OFF, but different functions are needed since it's a buzzer. Here's how to set it up in a new project in Thonny called "Buzzer":

from gpiozero import Buzzer

from time import sleep

Just like with LEDs, GPIO Zero needs to know which pin your buzzer is connected to for control. Specify this by adding the following line:

buzzer = Buzzer (15)

153

The code is similar to LED control, except now we're using a buzzer instead. Here's the code to make the buzzer buzz:

while True:

    buzzer.on()

    sleep(1)

    buzzer.off()

    sleep(1)

Press the green flag to start the buzzer buzzing. If you hear the buzzer clicking once per second, it's likely a passive buzzer. An active buzzer generates a rapidly changing signal to vibrate its metal plates, producing an oscillating sound.

Press the "Stop" button to close the program, but make sure the buzzer isn't buzzing at that moment, or it will continue buzzing until you rerun the program.

## Challenge: Improving the Buzz

To make the buzzer buzz for a shorter period of time, adjust the sleep duration in the code. To create a circuit that controls the buzzer with a button, you'll need to integrate button control into the code and adjust the circuit accordingly.

# PYTHON PROJECT 2 QUICK REACTION GAME

You can now use LEDs and buttons as devices to give and receive information. This allows you to create a real physical computing experience. One exciting application is a two-player quick-reaction game that determines who has the fastest reaction time. To complete this project, you will need the following materials: LEDs, a breadboard, a 330-ohm resistor, 2 push-button switches, and M2Fs and M2M jumper wires.

To begin, you need to build a circuit. Connect the left switch on your board to the GPIO 14 pin (labeled GP14 in Figure 6-7). Connect the second switch on the right side of the breadboard to the GPIO 15 pin (labeled GP15). For the LED, connect the longer leg to the 330-ohm resistor, and then connect the other end of the resistor to the GPIO 4 pin (labeled GP4) on your Raspberry Pi. Finally, connect the second leg of each component to the ground rail.

To complete the circuit, connect the ground rail to the Raspberry Pi's ground pin (labeled GND).

To begin, open Thonny and create a new project called "Reaction Game." We will need to use the button and LED functions from the GPIOZero library, as well as the sleep function. Import these functions by adding the following lines to the script section:

from gpiozero import LED, Button

from time import sleep

Next, we need to specify which pins the buttons and LED are connected to. Add the following lines:

led = LED (4)

right_button = Button (15)

left_button = Button (14)

Now, let's test if the LED is working correctly. We'll turn it on for 5 seconds and then turn it off. Add the following lines:

led.on()

sleep (5)

led.off ()

To add some randomness to the game, we can modify the sleep function to generate a random interval between 5 and 10 seconds. Import the `uniform` function from the `random` library by adding the following line:

from random import uniform

Replace the line `sleep (5) ` with `sleep (uniform (5, 10)) ` to use the random interval.

Now, when you run the program, the LED will stay lit for a random duration between 5 and 10 seconds. Each time you run the program, the duration will be different, adding unpredictability to the game.

To detect button presses from the players, we need to define a function. Scroll down to the end of the program and add the following code:

```
def pressed(button):

    if button.pin.number == 14:

        print (left_name + " won the game")

    else:

        print (right_name + " won the game")
```

Python uses indentation to identify lines that are part of a function. Thonny will automatically indent the second line for you.

Finally, we need to assign the `pressed` function to the `when_pressed` event handlers of the buttons. Add the following lines:

```
right_button.when_pressed = pressed

left_button.when_pressed = pressed
```

To play the game, run the program and press one of the buttons as soon as the LED turns off. The Python shell at the bottom of the Thonny window will display a message indicating which button should have been pressed.

To personalize the game, you can enter the names of the players. Below the line `from random import uniform`, add the following code:

left_name = input ("Left player name is: ")

right_name = input ("Right player name is: ")

Go back to the `pressed` function and replace the line `print(str(button.pin.number) + " won the game")` with the following lines:

if button.pin.number == 14:

   print (left_name + " won the game")

else:

   print (right_name + " won the game")

Run the program again and enter the names of the players in the Python shell. When a button is pressed, the corresponding player's name will be displayed instead of the pin number.

To handle the issue of multiple button presses, we will introduce a new function from the `sys` library called `exit`. At the end of the import line, add the following code:

from os import _exit

In the `pressed` function, below the line `print (right_name + " won the game")` `, add the following line:

_exit (0)

Make sure to indent `_exit (0)` with four spaces and align it with the `else` statement.

This will instruct Python to exit the program after the first button press, ensuring that the player who pressed the secondary button doesn't get any points for losing the game.

Your final program should look like this:

```
from gpiozero import LED, Button

from time import sleep

from random import uniform

from os import _exit

left_name = input ("Left player name is: ")

right_name = input ("Right player name is: ")

led = LED (4)

right_button = Button (15)

left_button = Button (14)

led.on()

sleep (uniform (5, 10))

led.off()

def pressed(button):

if button.pin.number == 14:

print (left_name + " won the game")
```

else:

print (right_name + " won the game")

_exit (0)

right_button.when_pressed = pressed

left_button.when_pressed = pressed

Run the program, enter the player names, and wait for the LED to turn off to see the winner's name. You will also see the message "Backend terminated (returncode: 0)" in the Python shell, indicating that the program has existed. Use the "Start/Stop" button to restart or stop the program.

Congratulations! You have successfully created your own physical game.

# CHALLENGE: ENHANCE THE GAME

Would you like to implement a loop to make the game run continuously? Remember to remove the _exit (0) command!

Additionally, how can you incorporate a score counter to keep track of the winner across multiple rounds? Did you know you can set a timer to measure your reaction time when the light goes off?

# VIRTUAL GAMING WITH RASPBERRY PI 5

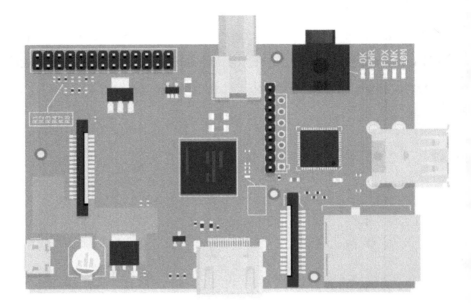

With the increasing popularity of mobile gaming and virtual gaming, massively multiplayer online (MMO) games with streaming and voice chat through headsets have become the latest trend. Experts predicted this trend years ago.

However, the unexpected surge in retro gaming is remarkable. No one anticipated that a credit card-sized single-board computer like the Raspberry Pi would play such a significant role in the revival of retro gaming. Building a retro gaming machine using the versatile Raspberry Pi is simple because it can emulate various gaming platforms.

To construct one, you'll need information about RetroPie ROMs, downloads, and other resources.

What are the requirements for building a Raspberry Pi Gaming Center?

Building a robust and capable Raspberry Pi retro gaming machine requires several components. Let's discuss the necessary hardware while keeping the software in mind.

- Raspberry Pi 5 board
- The Raspberry Pi

The Raspberry Pi has undergone multiple iterations since its release in 2012, with each version becoming more powerful and efficient than the previous one. Currently, there are two viable options:

1. Raspberry Pi 5: This model features a 1.5GHz 64-bit quad-core ARM Cortex-A72 system-on-a-chip (SOC) with up to 4GB LPDDR RAM (shared with the GPU). It measures 3.370 × 2.224 inches (85.60 × 56.5 mm) and has built-in 802.11b/g/n/ac wireless networking and Bluetooth.

2. Raspberry Pi Zero: This smaller device uses a 1GHz single-core ARM1176JZF-S SOC with 512MB RAM (shared with the GPU). It has a compact size of 2.56 × 1.18 inches (65 × 30 mm) and also has a wireless variant called the Zero W.

While the Pi 3B+ can handle the task, the Pi 5 offers better performance, so we recommend choosing this option.

# Other Hardware and Cables

Once you have your Raspberry Pi, there are a few additional items you'll need to get started, such as a reliable SD card, an HDMI cable, game controllers, a keyboard, and a mouse. If you opt for a Raspberry Pi 5 with 1GB of RAM, it shouldn't cost you more than $40. However, if you're starting from scratch, a complete kit should cost less than $100.

If you choose the Raspberry Pi with enhanced 4GB of RAM, it will be more expensive. You can purchase a starter kit that includes everything you need, except for the mouse and keyboard.

Once you have all the necessary hardware, you'll need to find the right emulators. It's recommended to install an emulation suite, but if you prefer, you can install the emulators individually. The emulation suite comes with many popular emulators and can be written to an SD card. There may also be other emulators preinstalled in the suite that are not listed.

## 1. RetroPie

RetroPie is perhaps the most popular retro gaming software for Raspbian. It offers a wide collection of emulators accessible through the user-friendly Emulation Station interface. While it includes several bundled ported games (games that can be played directly on the Raspberry Pi), the emulators themselves are available via RetroArch.

## 2. RecalBox

RecalBox supports over 40 emulators, including MAME, and offers access to over 30,000 titles. It also uses the Emulation Station interface and benefits from emulation support provided by RetroArch/libretro.

RecalBox enhances the gaming experience with features like cheat codes, a rewind tool to undo mistakes, and screenshot capabilities. Unlike RetroPie, RecalBox is only available as a writable microSD card image and cannot be manually installed. Both RecalBox and RetroPie include the option to install Kodi.

### 3. PiPlay

PiPlay is a compact alternative to RetroPie and RecalBox. It features 12 emulated machines and includes the ScummVM point-and-click adventure game platform. PiPlay can be downloaded and written to a disk or installed directly on the Pi through GitHub. It has a more traditional, text-based interface compared to the slick user interface of Emulation Station, but it offers stable emulation and good controller support.

### 4. Lakka

Lakka is marketed as a lightweight Linux distribution that turns a small computer into a full-fledged emulation console. It also utilizes RetroArch and provides access to around 40 emulators and thousands of games. Lakka allows you to upload game ROMs from a separate computer. Additionally, you can dual-boot Lakka with BerryBoot or NOOBS to run it alongside other Raspberry Pi operating systems.

### 5. Pi Entertainment System (PES)

PES is an Arch Linux-based collection of emulators bundled with RetroArch. It features 18 hardware platforms, including MAME. PES includes Kodi and supports various game controllers, including popular ones like the PS3 and PS4 control pads. It also provides wireless network and network gaming capabilities for retro platforms (excluding N64), and it can be dual-booted with BerryBoot.

### 6. Batocera

Batocera is an unusual retro gaming solution available for all Raspberry Pi models. It supports a wide range of gaming platforms, and all you need to do is plug in your game controller to start playing. Minimum configuration is required as everything comes pre-installed and enabled. Note that some platforms may not be available on the Pi, while versions for x86 devices offer a larger selection of emulators.

## Choosing the Right Emulation Suite

With a wide range of options available, it can be challenging to decide. If you're looking for a versatile system that can emulate a variety of platforms, both RecalBox and RetroPie are excellent choices. These two options are quite similar, so you can't go wrong with either of them.

However, if you're seeking a more specialized experience, you may want to consider Batocera, PiPlay, Lakka, or PES. These alternatives offer unique features and cater to specific preferences.

## Where to Find RetroPie ROM Downloads

To install games or applications on an emulator, you'll need ROMs. Both game ROMs and BIOS ROMs are necessary. It's important not to overlook the need for BIOS ROMs, as emulators cannot launch games without them. It's worth noting that ROMs for RetroPie are available both legally and illegally.

In the past, if you owned the original game, you could legally use the ROM. However, with the presence of peer-to-peer networking, even on some standard download websites, this practice has become risky.

One alternative is to create your own ROMs. Although the process may vary depending on the platform, it is still possible to find the necessary hardware. For example, you can purchase a USB device like the Commodore 64 Datasette (cassette player) to connect to your computer. We provide this information under the assumption that the ROM will be strictly used for personal purposes. Most of the required components can be found online.

## Adding ROMs to RetroPie and Other Suites

To add ROMs to your Raspberry Pi, you'll need to copy them to the correct directory. One convenient option is to use an FTP solution that supports SSH, such as FileZilla. Some emulation suites also offer a browser interface that allows you to upload ROMs directly from your computer.

Once you have the ROMs in place, navigating through your game library becomes easy. Most retro gaming suites provide a user-friendly library browser, allowing you to simply use your controller to select and launch games.

## Options for Retro Controllers: What Can You Use?

There are several controllers that are compatible with your Raspberry Pi retro gaming setup. While wired controllers generally provide the best performance, there are also reputable Bluetooth options available.

Controllers from the Sony PlayStation 3 and 4 can be connected to the Raspberry Pi. Additionally, controllers from the Xbox One, Xbox 360, and PlayStation 3 and 4 should all work. If you're interested in connecting an Xbox One controller to your Raspberry Pi, we have an article with more information on how to do that. If you're using an N64 emulator, a PS4 controller will also work with your Raspberry Pi retro gaming system.

For a more authentic retro gaming experience, you can opt for old-school joysticks and console controllers that have USB connectors. These are readily available. However, you may choose to use a retro console-themed case and proudly display it. There are plenty of designs available, such as the mini SNES console design.

If you're feeling creative, you can even explore 3D printing. Many retro-style cases can be found online as digital files, which you can purchase and produce yourself. If you don't have a 3D printer, there are services available where you can upload the design and have them print and ship it to you. If you plan to build your own case, you can take inspiration from the sleek designs of popular games.

Retro gaming is growing in popularity, and a Raspberry Pi combined with some effort can help you create amazing RetroPie game stations. Building a retro gaming rig with a library of ROMs is a straightforward and enjoyable project that provides endless gaming pleasure.

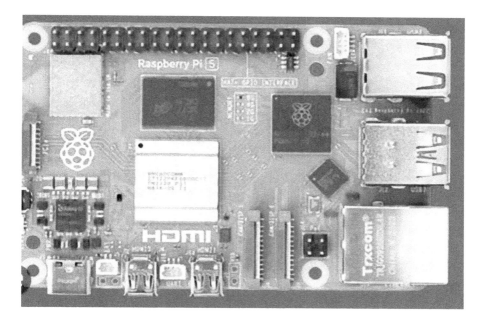

# RASPBERRY PI 5: Tips and Tricks

## *1. Overclocking:*

If you need a performance boost, consider overclocking your Raspberry Pi 5. Overclocking involves running the CPU at a higher clock speed than its default setting. However, be cautious as this can increase power consumption and heat generation, potentially reducing the lifespan of your device. Make sure to follow proper instructions and monitor the temperature closely.

- **Pros**: Improved processing power for demanding tasks.
- **Cons**: Increased power consumption, heat generation, and potential risk of reducing the lifespan of the device.

- **Caution:** Monitor temperature closely and ensure proper cooling.

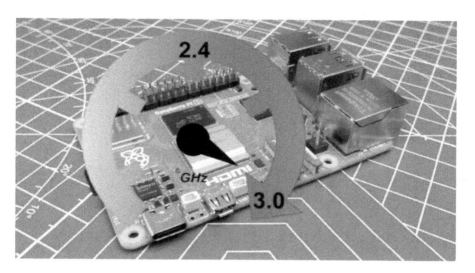

## 2. Use a High-Quality Power Supply:

A reliable power supply is essential for stable operation. Invest in a quality power adapter that provides a steady voltage and current to avoid issues like under-voltage warnings or system instability.

- **Pros**: Ensures stable operation and reduces the risk of damage to the device.

- **Cons**: Lower-quality power supplies may cause system instability or hardware damage.

- **Recommendation:** Invest in a power supply with appropriate specifications and certifications.

### 3. Active Cooling:

Since Raspberry Pi devices can generate heat during intensive tasks, consider adding active cooling solutions like a small fan or heatsink. This can help dissipate heat more effectively and prevent thermal throttling, which can degrade performance.

- **Pros**: Prevents thermal throttling, maintains optimal performance, and prolongs the lifespan of the device.

- **Cons:** Requires additional hardware and power consumption.

- ***Recommendation:*** Choose an appropriate cooling solution based on the intended usage and environmental conditions.

### 4. Update Firmware and Software:

Regularly update the firmware and software on your Raspberry Pi 5 to ensure you have the latest features, security patches, and bug fixes. You can use commands like `sudo apt update` and `sudo apt upgrade` to update the software packages.

- **Pros:** Improves system stability, security, and compatibility with software updates.
- **Cons:** May require internet access and system reboot.
- **Recommendation:** Schedule regular updates using package management tools like apt to keep the system up-to-date.

5. ***Expand Storage with USB Drives***: Although the Raspberry Pi 5 comes with built-in storage options, you can expand storage capacity by connecting USB drives or external hard drives. This is useful for storing large files, media libraries, or running applications that require more storage space.

- **Pros:** Increases storage flexibility and capacity beyond the built-in options.
- **Cons**: Requires additional hardware and may affect portability.
- **Recommendation:** Use high-speed and reliable storage devices for optimal performance.

## 6. SH Access:

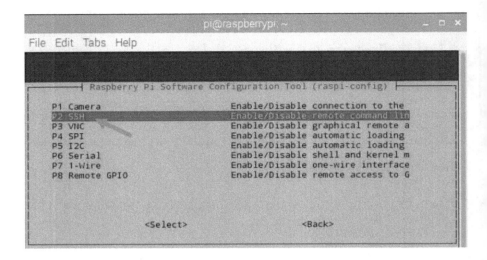

Enable SSH (Secure Shell) access to your Raspberry Pi 5 to remotely control it from another device on the same network. This allows you to perform tasks, transfer files, and troubleshoot issues without needing a physical monitor, keyboard, or mouse connected to the Pi.

- **Pros:** Facilitates remote administration, troubleshooting, and file transfer without physical access.

- **Cons**: Requires network configuration and security considerations.

- **Recommendation:** Secure SSH access with strong passwords or SSH keys and restrict access to trusted devices.

## 7. *Optimize for Performance*:

Configure your Raspberry Pi 5 for optimal performance by disabling unnecessary services and background processes. You can use tools like `raspi-config` to adjust settings such as GPU memory allocation, overclocking parameters, and boot options.

- **Pros:** Maximizes system resources and enhances overall performance.
- **Cons:** May require technical knowledge and experimentation.
- **Recommendation**: Use tools like raspi-config to adjust settings such as GPU memory allocation, overclocking, and boot options.

## 8. *Backup Your System:*

Regularly backup your Raspberry Pi 5 system to prevent data loss in case of hardware failure or software corruption. You can create disk images using tools like `dd` or use backup utilities like `rsync` to synchronize files between your Pi and another storage device.

- **Pros:** Safeguards critical data and configurations, streamlines recovery procedures.
- **Cons:** Requires storage space and periodic maintenance.
- **Recommendation**: Automate backup tasks using tools like dd, rsync, or dedicated backup utilities.

## 9. *Explore GPIO Pins:*

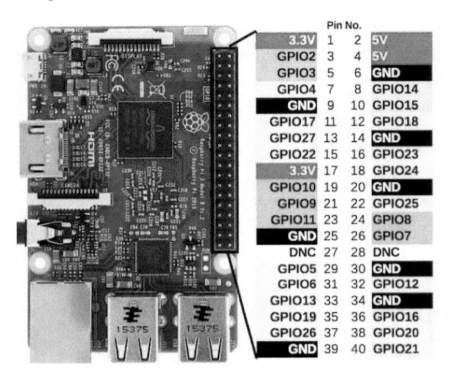

Raspberry Pi 5 comes with GPIO (General Purpose Input/Output) pins that allow you to connect and control external hardware such as sensors, LEDs, and motors. Explore the capabilities of GPIO pins by experimenting with various projects and interfacing with different components.

- **Pros:** Offers versatility and expandability for DIY projects and experimentation.
- **Cons:** Requires understanding of electronics and programming concepts.

- **Recommendation:** Refer to GPIO pinout diagrams and experiment with different components using programming languages like Python or dedicated libraries.

10. Explore Software Ecosystem: Take advantage of the vast software ecosystem surrounding Raspberry Pi 5. Explore diverse operating systems like Raspbian, Ubuntu, or specialized distributions tailored for specific purposes. Additionally, leverage a wide range of open-source applications, libraries, and community projects to expand the functionality of your Raspberry Pi 5.

- **Pros:** Access to diverse software solutions, educational resources, and community support.
- **Cons:** Choosing the right software for specific requirements may require research and testing.
- **Recommendation:** Explore available distributions, applications, and online resources to discover new possibilities and projects suited to your interests and needs.

By following these tips and tricks, you can enhance the performance, reliability, and versatility of your Raspberry Pi 5 for various projects and applications.